BE'ER HAGOLAH INSTITUTES

293 Neptune Avenue
Brooklyn, New York 11235

I did not come to this country to save myself or to seek positions of personal power," Rabbi Kotler said. "Rather, I am here so that, with your help, we can save our brothers and the centers of Torah learning all over Europe!"

"On the other side of the ocean our brothers are waiting for our help," he continued. "Only you, the Jews of America, are able to help them. Do it now! Save them!"

Rabbi Aharon Kotler, *To Save A World*, page 43

In our generation, thousands of Russian children are landing on American shores each year. And it is now up to us to make the sacrifices.

Be'er Hagolah Institutes was founded ten years ago to combat the forces that were preventing the ideals of Judiasm from reaching the *neshamos* of these innocent children. There are presently over 600 students studying at our school. This number is increasing dramatically each year as a result of the tremendous influx of new Soviet immigrants. Be'er Hagolah's outstanding staff of teachers, guidance counselors, family educators, and professionals offer a full range of educational programs for the students and their parents, as well as social experiences such as family *shabbatonim*, *chavrusa* programs with *bnei yeshivah*, Big Sister-Little Sister, Bais Yaakov programs, summer camping and countless other activities; all geared to introduce and inspire them to Torah living.

"Each generation must answer to a different test. Our generation will have to give testimony regarding what we did for Russian Jews.

Harav Hagaon R'Yaakov Kaminetsky *zt"l*

Whoever teaches another's son Torah is considered as having created him for it is written: "...and the souls whom they (Avrohom and Sara) created in Charan".

The genius of Ari Smith's short fruitful life was that he taught Torah to children who could learn from no one else. Because he thirsted for their knowledge, they learned; because he ached with their emptiness, they listened.

Ari was an original. He wasted little energy over reputation, status, image. He was humble and often apologetic, yet he labored with an iron persistence and indomitable will. His very presence conveyed Torah ideals to his Talmidim, and by bringing them Torah he captured their souls.

PROFILES IN HOLOCAUST RESCUE

TO SAVE A WORLD

VOLUME II

DR.
DAVID
KRANZLER

RABBI
ELIEZER
GEVIRTZ

Including:
The Children of Shefford
by Shari Schwartz

CIS PUBLISHERS

New York · London · Jerusalem

Published and distributed
in the U.S., Canada and overseas by
C.I.S. Publishers and Distributors
180 Park Avenue, Lakewood, New Jersey 08701
(908) 905-3000 Fax: (908) 367-6666

Distributed in Israel by
C.I.S. International (Israel)
Rechov Mishkalov 18
Har Nof, Jerusalem
Tel: 02-538-935

Distributed in the U.K. and Europe by
C.I.S. International (U.K.)
89 Craven Park Road
London N15 6AH, England
Tel: 01-809-3723

Book and cover design: Deenee Cohen
Typography: Nechamie Miller

ISBN 1-56062-088-9 hard cover
1-56062-089-7 soft cover

PRINTED IN THE UNITED STATES OF AMERICA

BE'ER HAGOLAH
"The School That Cares"

TO CARE: Webster's definition — Concern, attention, regard.

Be'er Hagolah is a unique school in performing its many services.

It provides it's incoming children with their first vital contact and training, and for many their first awareness, of Jewish tradition.

This school serves the Soviet Jewish Communtity, gearing itself to their special needs in so many diverse areas.

There are currently 65 faculty members, exclusive of principals and administrators. In addition to a full Hebrew and English studis staff, there are specialists in English as a Second Language, Computers, Art, Music and Honor's Math. The tone in programs offered is one of *professionalism and caring* to over 600 children.

Be'er Hagolah -
A Program rich in Torah Education *and*

Children:

Full scholarships for all new arrivals
*
Hands on program of Jewish laws and customs,
Jewish holidays, etc.
*
Hot lunches, bus transportation
*
Absorbtion program/E.S.L. program
*
Shabbatonim, chagigas, chavrusa program
*
One-on-one tutorial programs
*
Pre-med program - Mt. Sinai Hospital
*
Pre-law program
*
After school programs for public school students
*
After school homework programs
*
College advisor, Russian speaking social workers
*
Honors program in math
*
200 children attending various sleepaway camps in
the Catskill mountains
*
350 children in day camp - includes 100 public school
children
*
Evening sports, learning program

Secular Education for Soviet Immigrants

Adults:

Education classes

*

Family shabbatonim

*

Russian speaking family educators

*

***Kashruth* program**

*

Jewish festival programs

*

Outreach projects to parents of public school students

*

Full support system for Be'er Hagolah graduates

*

Adopt-a-Family

*

***Hachnosas Kallah* - weddings and family support**

*

***Yom Tov* retreats for the entire family**

*

Sunday morning beginner programs for children and their parents

*

Summer school for new immigrants wishing to get a "head start"on learning the English and Hebrew languages

*

***Yom Tov* Meals-on-Wheels**

An Inside Look

We bring the joy of the holidays to our students... perhaps for the very first time of their lives.

At Be'er Hagolah

"Each generation must answer to a different test. Our generation will have to give testimony regarding what we did for Russian Jews.

Harav Hagaon R'Yaakov Kaminetsky *zt"l*

The frequent presence of our great Torah leaders fills the hearts of our students with a love for our holy Torah.

TABLE OF CONTENTS

PROFILES IN HOLOCAUST RESCUE

TO SAVE A WORLD

INTRODUCTION

SHE WAS ONLY EIGHT YEARS OLD, BUT THOSE EIGHT YEARS already held a lifetime of experience.

Bina Lipschitz's lot had once seemed a pleasant one. The youngest of six children, securely nestled within the fold of her firmly observant family, she grew up in Vienna amid the enchantments of parks, gardens and frilly houses she fantasized into fairy tale castles. Only slowly did she notice the intrusions on her idyllic existence.

She couldn't remember when she had first heard the term Nazis. Her parents hadn't burdened her with political information, but she soon noticed the distaste with which they uttered the word. Then came new phrases: *Anschluss*, *Kristallnacht*, *Judenrein*, each evoking more fear than the other. Suddenly, it became dangerous for her beloved father, a proud Jew with beard and *peyos*, to leave the safety of their home. Her world was crumbling, and she had no idea why.

Thus, when her parents gravely gathered their children together and asked them to listen carefully, Bina sensed something ominous ahead. She was right. The children and their parents would soon be parted. It wasn't because they didn't love the children, her father had explained. It was precisely because they loved them so much that this was necessary.

The Nazis had taken over Austria, he explained, and were making life impossibly hard for Jews. Some men had been taken away to labor camps, and no one knew if they would ever return. And there was talk of a coming war that would certainly bring further calamity. The only solution was to leave the country, but that was very difficult. Very few countries were willing to take in Jews. However, he'd found out from a group called Agudath Israel that England would accept some Jews—young ones. A transport was being prepared to take Jewish children to new homes in that country. They would be placed in temporary homes, and their parents would join them as soon as they could. Then they'd all be together again. But meanwhile they'd be safe, and that was the important thing. As hard as the separation would be, it was the only thing to do.

Bina's oldest sister resisted; she wanted to stay with her parents, and her elder brother was learning in a *yeshivah* in Poland. The younger children, however, were sent off. Their father braved going outdoors and brought them to the point of departure. It was the first time that Bina had seen this usually cheerful man cry.

The trip remained a flurry of images: the children gathering at the train station in Vienna; arriving in Amsterdam and leaving by boat for England; being led through the mists of London to be placed in a new home so far from her real one.

The homesickness had lingered, intensified by the prospect of yet another separation since her siblings had been put up elsewhere. However, not all had gone badly. She had been taken in by a friendly Jewish family, and their two daughters had become her new companions. The parents had accepted her and given her attention, lots of attention.

Too much, in fact. The host family's daughters became jealous. Friction developed, followed by fights. There were conferences and discussions, but in the end, nothing helped. The parents were sorry. They'd tried to do a good deed, but it hadn't worked out. She would have to stay with someone else.

So now she stood, suitcase in her hand, on the doorstep of a man she didn't know, expected to make yet another transition in a life now filled with them. Who would this new guardian be? she wondered. And how long would it be before he, too, shunted her elsewhere?

"This house belongs to someone named Rabbi Schonfeld," her erstwhile host said, as if reading her mind. "He's in charge of these children's transports. He'll know where to place you." He rang the bell and took a step back.

A rabbi? A man with a long, white, flowing beard? What use would he have for someone as young as her?

Suddenly, the door opened, and Bina gasped. Facing her was a young man, impressively distinguished and tall as a mountain, with a dark, impeccably kept beard.

"Yes?" he called out in a resonant voice.

"She's from Vienna, and her name is Bina Lipschitz," the man accompanying Bina said. "I'm sorry I can't care for her any longer. I'm sure you'll do better." With that, he turned and disappeared into the night.

The rabbi stared for a moment at the girl who had been dropped at his doorstep, and then he smiled.

"Well, welcome, Bina," he said. "Come in, please."

He led her into the cluttered house and she looked around. There were other girls there, too, all older than her, smiling and animated. Their chatting suddenly ceased, as they focused their attention on the newcomer.

It was then that the full significance of the moment impacted upon her. Here she was, alone, without parents, without siblings, turned out twice, standing in a stranger's home, just one among so many, the youngest and newest in the crowd. She burst forth with a torrent of tears.

Rabbi Schonfeld acted quickly. He shooed the other girls away and had her sit down at the table opposite him. Putting some refreshments before her, he reassured her soothingly.

"Don't let the other girls frighten you, Bina," he said softly. "They've been through hard times, as I'm sure you have, and they're living here for a while until we can find places that fit them just right. Would you like to stay here, too? In fact, we have a bed that would be just the right size for you."

Bina looked up, but the tears still kept flowing.

"But we can discuss all that later," Rabbi Schonfeld said. "First, there's something else I'd like to ask you. Have you ever made a trip around London at night to see the sights? There are many interesting things to see, something new every time. Have you ever done that?"

Slowly, Bina's curiosity began pushing her fears aside. With war looming, gas was a rare commodity, and driving for pleasure was an unusual treat. She shook her head and muttered a small, "No."

"Well, you know what? With all the work I have to do here, helping to bring Jewish children over to England and finding them places to stay, I get a little restless. It's been a hard day, and I'd really like to get out and see what's new out there tonight. But I don't like travelling alone. I get a bit lonely. So would you do me a great big favor?"

Bina's eyes widened.

"Would you agree to come with me?"

The tears were by now past history. The girl nodded a vigorous yes.

"And I'll tell you what," the rabbi went on. "Since there's a little more room in the car, why don't we invite one more girl to go along? And I'll let you choose her."

Bina took warmly to the suggestion. For once, she would

make the decisions; she would be the kingmaker and acquire a new companion in the process. The girl she selected was one she had known slightly in Vienna, and the three set out on a happy journey together, virtually her first joyful excursion since she had left her parents.

The war years brought further dislocations for her, but she managed to take them in stride. Bina found a new home, reunited with her sisters, pursued an education, got a job and eventually settled in the United States. The traumas of the past still sorely rankled at times, but whenever she despaired, one image sustained her. A kindly man had put everything else aside and had showered personal interest on a lost and friendless girl who desperately needed it.

Someone had, miraculously, cared.

The Jews had few friends during the holocaust years. There were few who cared about what was happening to them, few who shared their suffering. And even among those who pitied them in their plight and denounced their tormentors, few took bold, active steps to help them—until it was too late.

What is especially infuriating about this inaction is that the Nazis made no pretense at disguising their intentions towards the Jews, even well before the start of World War II.

Throughout that war, Jews remained the main targets and victims of an enemy whose evil knew no bounds. The Nationalist Socialists, or Nazis, under Adolf Hitler *yemach shemo*, considered themselves the "Master Race." These Germans saw themselves as members of a naturally superior breed who deserved to control the world. With their mighty war machine, they conquered one European country after another, and came close to holding sway over almost the entire civilized world. Yet they reserved their fullest fury for the defenseless Jews.

For the Nazis, the Jew represented evil incarnate. In their

minds, the Jews were responsible for Germany's defeat in World War I and all its ensuing problems. This was true, according to Hitler's racist ideology, because Jews were biologically inferior to the blond-haired, blue-eyed Aryan "supermen." Therefore, said the Nazis, their very presence in Germany threatened to contaminate German culture, and they had to be forcibly removed from contact with Aryans. Since the Nazis considered Jews subhuman and racially inferior, there was no limit to the cruelty to which they could be subjected. As a result, Nazi soldiers felt justified in murdering them without a tinge of guilt. Thus, the Nazi persecution of the Jews was even more devastating than that applied by the Church. Here there was no option to escape through conversion. In the Nazis' eyes, Jews were inherently despicable, and there was nothing the Jews could do to get around it.

The persecution of German Jews began from the moment Hitler gained power in 1933. At first, the measures taken against them, while extremely painful, seemed to follow the usual pattern of European anti-Jewish sentiment: taunts, beatings and restrictions. Jews were barred from jobs and schools; Jewish shops were shut and Jewish property confiscated.

Then, on November 9, 1938, came the coordinated calamity known as *Kristallnacht*, or the Night of the Broken Glass. On this horrendous night, Nazi hooligans—with full official approval—burned and destroyed almost two hundred *shuls* throughout Germany and Austria, destroyed over seven thousand Jewish businesses and homes, and murdered numerous Jews in cold blood. Twenty thousand other Jews were soon sent to slave labor camps like Dachau and Buchenwald. Then, adding insult to injury, the Nazis fined the Jews one billion marks (four hundred million dollars) for the destruction. In practice, this meant that no Jew could leave Germany without proof that he had paid his "share" of the enormous fine.

Now there could be no doubt that the Nazi threat to the

Jews was singularly monstrous. And yet, *Kristallnacht*, for all its fury, marked only the beginning.

Over the next seven years, until they were defeated in 1945, the Nazis kept expanding the limits of unimaginable brutality against their chief victims. When the war was at its height, the Nazi high command decided on what they called "the Final Solution to the Jewish Problem." The aim was the total degradation and destruction of Jewry. To the bitter end, the Nazis pursued this policy with an unwavering, pathological intensity.

The noose was tightened ever so cunningly. Jews were first expelled from their homes, then isolated, then imprisoned in ghettos like Lodz, Vilna, Bialystock and Warsaw. Finally, they were shipped off to the most terrifyingly efficient killing machines ever devised by depraved minds. Death camps like those at Auschwitz-Birkenau, Treblinka and Sobibor became chilling evidence of the bestial depths to which the Germans had sunk.

Even in 1944, when it became clear that the Nazis were losing the war, they did not relent in their attacks on the Jews. Instead, they stepped them up and sought out victims previously left unharmed. This effort cost the Nazis the use of soldiers and trains that were urgently needed elsewhere on the war front. They didn't care. In their mad, blind hatred of the Jews, the Nazis personified Amalek, the Jews' eternal enemy.

In the end, some six million holy Jewish souls—over a third of the Jews living at that time—perished at the hands of the Nazis and their supporters.

Over a million of them were children.

They would never have the chance to build families of their own; they would never know a life of adult achievement. The Torah that they might have mastered remained unlearned, and the *mitzvos* they might have done went unperformed. They were all, sadly, might-have-beens. And the children and grandchildren they might have had were lost to the world.

Each life lost was a tragedy all its own.

It should be remembered, though, that the Nazis did not massacre the Jews suddenly, overnight. The killings took place over several years, in several countries. Had they been stopped or slowed at any time along the way, at least hundreds of thousands of lives could have been saved.

Why weren't they? Why didn't the people of the free world act to stop the mass murders?

To be sure, the Nazis did all they could to keep their horrible crimes as secret as possible. They hid the death camps in isolated areas and reported nothing about the mass killings. Jews sent to the camps were often forced to write postcards to their relatives back home, assuring them that all was well. Those were usually their last written words before they were killed. All these efforts created a smoke screen over what the Nazis were really doing. And even many who suspected that something terrible was happening to the Jews could not believe just how terrible the situation really was.

Nevertheless, this excuse for inaction is not fully acceptable. It was clear from the very beginning of Hitler's rule that the Nazi regime would single the Jews out for brutal treatment. Any doubts about this were erased by the savagery of *Kristallnacht*. This public display of anti-Jewish hatred was obvious to all.

Later, the restriction of Jews to ghettos and their eventual deportation to concentration camps were publicized by the anti-Nazi underground. Even the mass murders, so well hidden by the Nazis, came to the attention of free world leaders after a few individuals escaped from the ghettos and death camps and told of their experiences. A report of mass deportation and murder of Jews from the Warsaw Ghetto was sent to Jewish leaders as well as Allied governments. And in

1944, detailed reports of the horrors of Auschwitz, as well as a plea to bomb the railroad lines to the camp, were spread throughout the free world.

The Allies, then, had a good inkling of what the Nazis were doing to the Jews, even if the full nature of their crimes remained unknown. And still, they did very little to stop the carnage.

It can be argued that rescue operations during the war were extremely difficult. For one thing, the Allies were deeply involved in fighting the war and needed all their resources to defeat the Nazis. Perhaps they didn't have the time or the means to save the Jews. In addition, the Jews were under the thumb of the Nazis, in Nazi-occupied territory, and the Allies had no way of freeing them.

All this must be taken into account. However, it must also be remembered that by mid-1944, the Allies were in complete control of the skies and could easily have bombed the railroad tracks leading to Auschwitz, with few if any risks (see Volume I, Chapter 1). Yet, it was never done. Clearly, the Allies did not give high priority to this act on behalf of trapped Jews.

More to the point, a few courageous groups and individuals showed that, when there was a concentrated effort, Jews *could* indeed be saved—without endangering the overall struggle against the Nazis. And many of these rescuers were not even Jewish.

The most noteworthy example of this involved the nation of Denmark. When the Nazis occupied Denmark and ordered that the Jews there begin wearing the yellow Star of David, Danish citizens reacted with revulsion. Showing their solidarity with the embattled Jews, they, too—starting with the Danish monarch, King Christian X—began wearing the Star.

Later, when the Nazis tried to arrest and deport Denmark's seven thousand two hundred Jews in 1943, the Danes warned them of the impending threat. Then they carried out a bold and complex rescue scheme, smuggling almost all the Danish Jews out overnight to safety in neutral Sweden on *Erev Rosh Hashanah*. When they came back to Denmark after the war, the Jews found their old homes preserved exactly as they had left them, awaiting their return.

Among individuals, the Swedish diplomat Raoul Wallenberg and his Swiss counterpart Karl Lutz showed how effectively bold persons could counter the Nazis' designs. In astonishing displays of bravery and defiance, they stopped the Nazis from sending thousands of Hungarian Jews to the Auschwitz death camp, claiming they had official Swedish or Swiss protection. Similarly, the Catholic German businessman Oskar Schindler saved hundreds of Jews during the war by insisting on employing them in his factory. And in occupied France, Pastor Andre Trocme helped make the Protestant village of Le Chambon into a mountain hideout for a thousand Jews.

Numerous other non-Jews risked—and sometimes lost— their lives by hiding Jews in their homes and providing for their welfare. Many of these have since been honored as *chassidei umos haolom* (righteous gentiles) at the Yad Vashem Memorial in Israel.

Unfortunately, these were among the few exceptions. The vast majority of nations and citizens of the world did little to help Jews, even when they had the opportunity to do so.

A prime reason for this apathy is that many European countries had a long history of anti-Semitism and oppressing their Jews. Their governments and people considered Jews unwanted foreigners and enemies of Christianity. Therefore, when the Nazis conquered these lands and instituted anti-Jewish measures, the local populations rarely protested. They often cooperated fully with the Nazis by helping round up and identify their Jewish neighbors. In some countries, like Romania, they went even further, rivaling the Nazis in their savage mistreatment of the Jews.

Even those countries that did not sanction anti-Jewish violence helped seal the doom of Europe's Jews through hard-hearted inaction—namely, their refusal to let endangered Jewish refugees set foot on their soil.

Between 1933 and 1941, many European Jews still had a chance to leave their native countries before harm overtook them. In the early years of the Nazi regime, the government's plan was to rid Nazi territory of Jews by forcing them to emigrate. However, there was a catch. Other nations had to be willing to accept the Jews. Most responded by shutting their doors tight, to keep the outsiders away.

When the representatives of thirty-two nations met at Evian, France, in 1938, to discuss the refugee problem, the conference room was filled with sympathetic rhetoric. But when the delegates came to the bottom-line question of who would take in the hapless victims, there was sudden silence. In the end, only one country declared itself interested in accepting the refugees: the Dominican Republic, a small nation in Central America. And only one place in the whole world, a section of Shanghai, China, permitted entry without restriction to thousands of Jews fleeing Hitler's wrath. Ironically, Shanghai was at the time controlled by Hitler's ally Japan.

Even the United States, despite its reputation as a symbol of freedom and liberty, severely limited Jewish immigration to its shores. There were strict quotas on the number of Europeans that would be allowed in, and these quotas remained intact throughout the war, even during the days of the Jews' greatest need. Between 1938 and 1941, when Jews were still able to leave Germany and German-occupied Austria, the United States admitted only one hundred fifty thousand European immigrants (non-Jews as well as Jews), even though the quotas allowed for two hundred twelve thousand. In 1943, the total was only twenty-four thousand—the lowest in eighty years.

In 1939, Hitler allowed nine hundred German Jews to leave on a ship, the *St. Louis*. In effect, he was daring the world, "You're complaining about my treatment of Jews. Let's see how eager you are to accept them yourselves." As the ship lurched from port to port along the Atlantic coast, the United States—along with Cuba, Columbia and Chile—turned them away. The passengers were on the verge of desperation when Holland, Belgium, England and France finally agreed to take them in. However, many of the passengers eventually lost their lives anyway when the Nazis occupied most of these lands.

Franklin Delano Roosevelt, President of the United States from 1933 to 1945, had many Jews among his close advisors. During his election campaigns, he had won the overwhelming support of Jewish voters. In many ways, he showed himself to be a great humanitarian and a gifted leader who skillfully overcame the opposition of American isolationists to guide America through the war.

Nevertheless, he did very little to push for rescue efforts on behalf of trapped European Jews. This powerful leader put politics ahead of humanitarian goals and decided not to challenge the large number of anti-Jewish and anti-immigration Americans. (A poll taken before the war noted that seventy seven percent of the public were opposed to allowing in additional Jewish immigrants from Europe.) Only late in the war, as a result of pressure from some Jews, did he take action, creating the War Refugee Board to help rescue Jews. He also finally agreed to establish a temporary haven for refugees at Oswego, New York, in January, 1944. The number of refugees allowed in? A total of nine hundred eighty four. Had Roosevelt acted earlier, and more boldly, he would have accomplished a great deal more.

Like the Americans, the British were at the forefront of the battle against the Nazis. They deserve credit for taking in some sixty thousand German Jewish refugees during the

1930s. (For a while, though, many of these Jews were sent to internment camps, suspected of being German spies. There, they often found themselves imprisoned side by side with actual Nazis.)

However, England also barred the way to the natural haven for Jews fleeing Europe—Eretz Yisrael. Though their fellow Jews in the Holy Land were willing to accept all of Hitler's intended victims, the British actively prevented Jews from arriving there. This harsh policy was the result of pressure from the Arabs, whose good will England sought because of its need for oil. Thus, in regard to Eretz Yisrael, England sided with the Arabs, most of whom openly supported Hitler, and against the Jews, with whom they shared a common hatred of the Nazis.

Aside from the refugee issue, both the Americans and the British could have helped the Jews by bombing the railroad tracks to Auschwitz. Had this happened, the daily transfer of thousands of Jewish victims to the death camps by train could easily have been slowed or even stopped. Only a few planes could have accomplished this task. There would have been little danger involved, since by then the Allies had virtual control of the skies. However, nothing was ever done.

In the final analysis, at the root of this international inertia lay official apathy, bureaucratic red tape and, at times, basic anti-Jewish feelings. The world didn't really care what was happening to the Jews. Hardly any nation wished to end their suffering by taking them in. Later, when the death camps were liberated and people saw what the Nazis had done, there was widespread sympathy for the Jews. But for the six million dead, sympathy was no longer any good.

The apathy of non-Jewish governments and individuals toward the plight of European Jewry was certainly tragic. But even more painful was the lack of forceful action taken by those who might have been expected to do anything to help—their fellow Jews in the free world.

Did they display a sense of responsibility to their endangered Jewish brothers and sisters? Even within the narrow parameters of the available options, did they do enough to help save those entrapped in Europe?

Sadly, not really.

Today, protest marches and demonstrations are commonplace. However, during the European Jews' years of agony, such public protests on their behalf were extremely rare. After the United States entered the conflict in 1941, there were a few rallies at Madison Square Garden and a few days of public fasting and prayer. And throughout the entire period, there was only one march in Washington—led by Orthodox rabbis—to bring attention to their plight. For the most part, though, while thousands of Jews were dying each day in Europe, the Jews in America, England, Switzerland and other free countries went about their daily routines with almost a business-as-usual attitude. Many of these Jews preferred to portray the war as an international conflict, instead of a drive against the Jews. It was not their intention to stand out in the crowd.

They therefore assumed a "hush-hush" approach of keeping mum about Jewish troubles. This stance was adopted by many Jewish leaders, including Rabbi Stephen Wise, an important Reform rabbi and head of the American Jewish Congress, World Jewish Congress and American Zionist Emergency Committee—in other words, the most prominent Jewish leader in America at this time. He worshipped President Roosevelt and his New Deal as proponents of the messianic age, and time and again he showed he would do anything to spare the President embarrassment.

Therefore, when the State Department asked him in 1942 to keep quiet about a report that European Jews were being massacred, he did so—for ten full weeks. He also ordered leading Jewish organizations to follow his lead. During this time, some one million additional Jews were killed.

Eventually, under prodding by the Orthodox, Wise and others did publicize the report, called for action to help the Jews and a delegation finally met briefly with Roosevelt on the issue in December, 1942. Yet, there was little of the driving urgency in their words and actions that might have produced greater results.

The effectiveness of leading secular American Jewish groups during the war has also been questioned. Controversy especially centers around the role played by the American Joint Distribution Committee in aiding European Jewry.

This organization, commonly known as the JDC, or the Joint, was by far the leading Jewish aid group at this time. It had enormous financial and political resources and was instrumental in sending million of dollars in assistance to European Jews. Certainly, the Joint's charitable efforts were most commendable, and many of its leaders were indeed well-meaning.

However, there were significant limits to the Joint's generosity. Its directors flatly refused to send any form of aid when that involved breaking governmental law. Normally, that would seem a commendable policy. But it was strictly enforced even when the result was a great loss of Jewish life.

For instance, when the United States declared war on Japan in late 1941, hundreds of *yeshivah* students and other Jews were left stranded in Shanghai, China (then controlled by Japan—see Volume I, Chapter 4). Up to this point, the Joint had been providing substantial aid to the Shanghai Jewish community. However, as soon as America banned all communications between the United States and Japan, that aid abruptly stopped. Most of the sixteen thousand Jewish refugees in Shanghai faced starvation, but the Joint's policy remained inflexible.

Why were Stephen Wise, the leaders of the Joint and other American Jews so hesitant to press the issue of Jewish suffering and challenge the government? Partly, it can be attributed to insecurity. For American Jews, by and large, full acceptance as equals in American society was their first priority. They therefore didn't want to risk being called disloyal foreigners by making the war a Jewish issue.

Certainly, the mood of pre-war America was not favorably disposed towards Jews. A poll during this time showed that fully twenty-four percent of those asked considered Jews to be a "menace to America," and fifty-six percent thought that "Jews have too much power in the United States." Demagogues like Father Charles Coughlin and Fritz Kuhn of the German-American Bund spoke to large, approving audiences of the "Jewish threat"; and those of the American First Committee, especially aviation hero Charles Lindbergh, warned that Jews were trying to get America involved in the overseas war. In such an atmosphere, most secular Jewish leaders were unwilling to press the government to save European Jewry.

However, not everyone was deterred by these fears. Consider the approach of a group called Vaad Hatzalah.

The Vaad had been founded in 1939 by Rabbi Eliezer Silver, an American Orthodox rabbi in Cincinnati who was a founder and leader of Agudath Israel and the Union of Orthodox Jewish Congregations of America. Its formation was urged by Rabbi Chaim Ozer Grodzenski, the great sage of Vilna, to aid the *yeshivah* students streaming into Vilna to escape the Nazi and Communist threats in Poland. Later, both Rabbi Avraham Kalmanowitz and Rabbi Aharon Kotler joined Rabbi Silver at the helm of the Vaad, immediately after their respective arrivals in America.

The Vaad's membership consisted mainly of recently-arrived European immigrants and American *baalei batim*, who were far from wealthy. The Vaad therefore never enjoyed the vast financial resources that the Joint had at its disposal. Nevertheless, it was able to assist and even rescue hundreds of thousands of European Jews during the war, including those stranded in Shanghai. To do so, the leaders of the Vaad sought any and all means available to keep the funds flowing, despite government restrictions. Together with other Orthodox rescue activists, especially Zeirei Agudath Israel under Elimelech Tress, they managed to channel the aid through neutral Switzerland with the help of the Polish government-in-exile. This method may have been technically illegal at the time, but it fulfilled a higher law, that of preserving human lives.

Why were the leaders of the Vaad willing and able to overcome obstacles to aiding trapped Jews, while those of the Joint and other secular Jewish organizations were not?

Basically, it boils down to a difference in priorities.

By the 1930s, most American Jews had turned their backs on the sacred commandments of the Torah. This included not only laws like *Shabbos* and *kashrus*, but also the Torah's sweeping moral values and its teachings about *Klal Yisrael's* unique identity. Rather than seeing the Jewish nation as a Chosen People bound to G-d's dicta, they preferred to be seen as well-integrated citizens of their country. Now looking and acting like the average non-Jew, they longed for full acceptance into the prevailing non-Jewish society. They dearly wished to be treated like equals with the gentiles, gaining entrance to their neighborhoods and country clubs and winning their friendship and respect. Nothing would have pleased them more than fitting seamlessly into the fabric of American society, minus all the identification marks of Judaism.

So when the government put restrictions on sending aid overseas, they went out of their way to comply. The needs of European Jews came second to their need to display national loyalty. They would go to any means to avoid standing out. They didn't clamor for Jewish immigration, for fear that the "old-fashioned European" newcomers would brand all Jews with the stigma of being different. And they looked down on such time-tested tactics as ransom and bribing officials to win the release of Jewish victims. Such measures were degrading, not befitting modern Jews in a modern world.

The Orthodox had a different perspective. They still used Hashem's Torah and the teachings of their Sages as their guides to life. And they knew the top priority assigned to Jewish survival and well-being. That survival could only be achieved through a commitment to one's fellow Jews. *"Kal Yisrael areivim zeh lazeh"*—All Jews are responsible for one another, the Sages insisted. For the the Jewish people to thrive, they had to pursue *areivus*, responsibility and unity, in building a sense of *klal*, community.

Jews therefore had to be their brothers' keepers, especially if those brothers were in mortal danger. *"Lo saamod al dam reiacha"*—Do not stand idly by while your brother's blood is being spilled,"instructed the Torah (*Vayikra* 19:16). In cases of *pikuach nefesh*—where lives are in peril—the Torah itself requires all-out action. Even the strictest prohibitions fall by the wayside in the cause of rescue. To the Orthodox, their mission was crystal clear. Nothing must stand in the way of saving European Jewry.

As a result, the leaders of the Orthodox rescue efforts sought out any and all avenues to help their fellow Jews escape the Nazis. They didn't care if bribery or sending messages via the Polish diplomatic code to bypass the State Department censor was scorned by others, just so long as it worked. If the government put obstacles in the way of aid, then these obstacles had to be surmounted. What was important was to leave no stone unturned in the attempt to aid others. And that aid wasn't limited to other religious Jews. The leading Orthodox rescue activists made a point of assisting *any* fellow Jew, no matter what his personal ideology. This stemmed from their appreciation of *areivus*. All Jews are members of an extended family, and all family members must be preserved.

This should not imply that *all* religious Jews of the free world were involved in rescue activities. That was as untrue as claiming that no irreligious Jews helped. The majority of the *frum* Jews at the time simply did not have the opportunity, means or initiative to put aside their own daily needs and devote themselves to *hatzalah*.

Fortunately, though, there *were* shining exceptions to the norm. These were special Jews who took extraordinary measures to help their fellow Jews during their time of gravest peril. Their numbers included Jews of all varieties and backgrounds. But a good proportion of these unique individuals were steeped in Torah values. They shared the Torah-taught view that saving Jewish lives took priority over all other concerns.

They are the subject of the *To Save a World* series.

The *To Save a World* series focuses on outstanding Orthodox activists who performed remarkable feats of relief and rescue during and after the holocaust years. The previous volume profiled Rabbi Michoel Ber Weissmandl, Rabbi Avraham Kalmanowitz, Reb Elimelech ("Mike") Tress, Mr. George Mantello, Mrs. Recha Sternbuch and Mrs. Renee Reichmann. In this second volume, we deal with their illustrious co-workers: Rabbi Aharon Kotler and Rabbi Eliezer Silver, outstanding Torah giants who, as leaders of the American-based Vaad Hatzalah rescue organization, labored tirelessly to aid and rescue Jews stranded in Europe; Dr. Yaakov Griffel, whose *hatzalah* efforts in Turkey and Eretz Yisrael helped save thousands of his Jewish brothers and sisters; Rabbi Shlomo Schonfeld, who rescued over three thousand Jews and brought them to England; and Rebbetzin Judith Grunfeld, whose sensitivity to the needs of refugees restored many of them to full spiritual health, especially the children she cared for in the small English village of Shefford. They all had distinct methods of dealing with the crises brought on by the war. Yet, at the same time, as Orthodox Jews they all shared a common perspective of the overriding importance of rescue work. (We have also added a brief survey of the Holocaust and a chronology for the benefit of those readers not fully familiar with the relevant historical events.)

The Rambam wrote, "There is no *mitzvah* as great as that of redeeming captives." Rav Yosef Colon (the Maharik) noted, "Unnecessary delay in ransoming a captive is as great a sin as murder." The Orthodox rescue activists therefore committed themselves with all the resources at hand to performing the *mitzvos* of *pidyon shevuyim* (rescuing hostages) and *hatzalas nefashos* (saving lives).

Consequently, the personalities of this series became part of a small, worldwide network of Jews devoted to rescue. Though most were unaware of the others before the war, the common crisis brought them in touch with one another. Eventually, many exchanged ideas and information.

Thus, when Rabbi Weissmandl needed someone to communicate his warnings about the Nazis and to put pressure on the American government to act, he turned to the Sternbuchs, as well as Dr. Griffel, who in turn contacted the Vaad Hatzalah and Agudath Israel. And when Rabbi Kalmanowitz, Rabbi Kotler and Rabbi Silver needed a way to send much-needed funds to Mirrer Yeshivah students stranded in Shanghai, they relied on the Sternbuchs in neutral Switzerland or Mr. Hans Lehmann in neutral Sweden to do so. Rabbi Weissmandl showed that Nazis could be bribed to free Jews, and Mrs. Sternbuch used the same tactic to help save a trainload of Jews headed for Auschwitz. And when the Sternbuch family pioneered the use of Latin American papers to protect Jews, George Mantello and later Dr. Yaakov Griffel, and even some secular organizations, expanded on the idea in a way that saved many thousands. Clearly, these leaders succeeded where others failed because of their ability to pool their resources in a united effort.

However, their work often remained difficult and dangerous. Throughout the war, these leaders put themselves at great personal risk through their rescue efforts. Sometimes they suffered severe setbacks. Recha Sternbuch was arrested and put on trial for smuggling Jews across the Swiss border and bribing guards to cooperate. Rabbi Kalmanowitz was tailed by the FBI; Rabbi Schonfeld was fired at by snipers. And Rabbi Weissmandl, who operated right under the Nazis' noses, was jailed more than once and was actually put on a train bound for Auschwitz. He managed to escape, but the rest of his family did not.

Nevertheless, these activists persisted. This is one key element that set them apart from many of their fellow Jews, religious or not. They shared a keen, farsighted grasp of the situation that eluded others. This enabled them to realize, where so many others did not, that with the Nazis overrunning Europe and trapping Jews, a business-as-usual attitude was unacceptable.

Instead, they turned the task of saving Jews into a twenty-four-hour-a-day crusade. These leaders forsook their normal lives and devoted all their resources and energies to rescue work. If that meant spending weeks away from their homes and families, or phoning diplomats at two o'clock in the morning, then that is what they did. They knew that if they put off the job, they might not have a second chance to finish it later.

What they accomplished was indeed remarkable. Though they were not experienced diplomats, and though they lacked extensive resources, their achievements were considerable. During the difficult war years, they raised millions of dollars for the rescue and relief of refugees—a huge sum at a time when the dollar was worth twenty or thirty times its value today, and when the average weekly paycheck was only twenty-five to thirty-five dollars.

Furthermore, these Orthodox Jews managed to establish

valued contacts with officials at the highest levels of government. Often they came up with creative, daring plans to aid those snared by Nazis. Rabbi Schonfeld, for instance, developed the idea of buying a whole island as an official haven for persecuted Jews. And Rabbi Weissmandl devised a scheme that, had others cooperated more, might have ransomed most of Europe's remaining Jews.

In the end, they played a leading role in the rescue of hundreds of thousands of Jews, caring for both their physical and spiritual needs. They also failed frequently, wholly or in part, and yet, even the failures are important as indications of great effort. A Jew is expected to make an effort towards rescue; success is in the hands of the Almighty.

Commenting on why Moshe Rabbeinu deserved to become Hashem's emissary in delivering the Jews from Egypt, Rabbi Aharon Kotler remarked that Moshe epitomized two sterling qualities. On the one hand, he was a natural leader, someone who could command men, stand up to enemies and rise to challenges. At the same time, he was a shepherd by instinct, a concerned father figure who was sensitive to the needs of every individual in his flock.

Such a person is fit to lead Hashem's holy people. And such were the activists who tended to their besieged nation during its darkest hour.

May the story of their efforts help us value the preciousness of every holy Jewish life.

THE HOLY FIRE OF TORAH

RABBI AHARON KOTLER

Rabbi Aharon Kotler, originally *rosh yeshivah* of Kletzk, Poland, was one of the greatest Torah leaders to settle in the United States as a result of the Holocaust. Upon his arrival in the United States in 1941, he became a fiery leader of Agudath Israel and Vaad Hatzalah, and he established the Lakewood Yeshivah, which would become the foremost Torah center in the world.

1 THE HOLY FIRE OF TORAH

RABBI AHARON KOTLER

THEIR FACES WERE STUDIES IN CURIOSITY, ANTICIPATION AND even, in some cases, boredom. As they stood observing the comings and goings at New York's Pennsylvania Station that spring day in 1941, they weren't sure of what would happen. They had no inkling whatsoever that they were about to witness a major turning point in American Jewish history.

The young men had been pressed into service by their mentor in Zeirei Agudath Israel, Elimelech ("Mike") Tress. "Come, we're going down to greet a true giant of our times," he had urged them.

Images of celebrities, such as famous sports personalities, immediately tantalized the minds of these very Americanized youngsters. They begged Mike to tell them whom they would be meeting.

"Rabbi Aharon Kotler," was the answer.

The name drew an overwhelmingly blank response. Few had even vaguely heard of him, and no one knew just who he was.

"Rabbi Kotler is one of the greatest *talmidei chachamim* of our times," Tress explained, trying to whip up enthusiasm. "For years he headed the famous *yeshivah* in Kletzk. Now he's made a miraculous escape from Europe to Japan via Russia, and he's just arrived in the United States. He deserves our warm welcome."

Then, peering intently at his young charges, he gently reminded them, "You know, sports heroes are fine, but for Torah Jews, the real heroes are Torah leaders."

So they had submitted to his coaxing and arrived at the mammoth train station, comprising a significant segment of the welcoming party. Suddenly, a swelling buzz indicated that something was occurring. The youngsters craned their necks as a dignified elder alighted from the train. Many recognized him as Rabbi Eliezer Silver, president of both Agudath Israel and Agudath Harabbanim, and a familiar veteran of the American Jewish scene.

Then someone else appeared at his side. He bore a graying brown beard, and he was slight and short, almost frail—notably unprepossessing.

Was this Rabbi Kotler? they wondered. Was this the "giant" they were to greet as a hero?

They listened politely as Rabbi Silver stepped up to the assembled throng and briefly introduced his colleague, calling him "the greatest Torah teacher of our generation."

Then Rabbi Silver drew back, and like a general impatient for the momentum of battle, Rabbi Kotler strode forward to make his remarks.

He spoke abruptly, in quick, machine gun-like bursts that made it hard for even the youngsters who knew Yiddish to understand him. Yet, even those who had no idea what he was saying were soon mesmerized by his presence. His manner of speaking showed that he was a man in a hurry, eager to gain results. And his eyes, a blazing blue, seemed to bore into each spectator, demanding not glory or honor but action, response and allegiance to a holy cause.

"On the other side of the ocean our brothers are waiting for our help," he began. "Only you, the Jews of America, are able to help them. Do it now! Save them!"

His opening comments immediately fired up the crowd. Those who had not understood were eagerly asking for a translation, and those who had were readily providing it.

"I did not come to this country to save myself or to seek positions of personal power," Rabbi Kotler continued. "Rather, I am here so that, with your help, we can save our brothers and the centers of Torah learning all over Europe!"

He went on: The American Jewish community had done admirable rescue work until now, but that work had to be expanded, and intensified. America must help, because America had the means and the manpower to save countless lives. The future of Torah now lay in the United States; there was a real potential for a great Jewish community there. Together, they would build a Torah center in this country that had once been dismissed as a "*treife medinah*". But first the Torah scholars of Europe had to be saved, and their holy traditions had to be preserved. There was no time to waste. The Jews of America had to invest all their wealth and their energy in a full-fledged rescue effort, beginning immediately!

"And I will offer my full services in any capacity to help," he concluded. "Whatever is necessary, whatever is needed, I will do. Starting this very minute!"

The assembled audience was galvanized. Clearly, here was someone who could rouse a complacent army, a commander who could build Orthodoxy into a viable force on seemingly alien soil.

Even the youngsters in the crowd sensed that Orthodox rescue efforts in America were about to shift into higher gear, and they, too, wanted to get more involved. Reb Aharon would inspire both them and their elders. And the work of Vaad Hatzalah, the rescue organization founded by Torah leaders like Rabbi Silver and later bolstered by Rabbi Avraham Kalmanowitz and others, would soar higher with the infusion of Rabbi Kotler's energy and wise guidance.

The crowd dispersed, feeling uplifted. But Reb Aharon wasn't content to leave them with only inspirational words.

The next morning, many of the dignitaries who had attended the welcome received a phone call.

"Kotler here," said the voice on the phone.

They were pleased to hear from him again. Was he offering his appreciation for the greetings, or offering his impressions of America? Not quite.

"What I want to know is this," Reb Aharon went on. "What has been done for rescue since we met yesterday?"

The day would come when this diminutive giant would revolutionize the future of Torah learning in the United States, and revitalize Orthodox Judaism throughout the world. As the founder and dean of Beth Medrash Govoha in Lakewood, New Jersey, he would emphatically show that Torah could indeed blossom in America in all its glory. The rabbi whose name meant nothing to even Orthodox American Jews in 1941 would be mourned by hundreds of thousands upon his death two decades later.

For the immediate present, though, he would be concerned with salvaging whatever he could of the European Torah community he had regretfully left behind. It was his holy mission, and he would carry it out relentlessly, as if the future of the world depended on it. Because, as he so well knew, it did.

A YOUTH OF PROMISE

The nineteenth century produced many notable *talmidei chachamim*, but only a select few achieved legendary status. One of these was the immortal Rabbi Chaim Soloveitchik, commonly called Reb Chaim Brisker. As a leader of the world famous Volozhiner Yeshivah, he had occasion to gauge the spiritual and academic potential of thousands of gifted *talmidim*. He was not one to toss off unwarranted praise. Yet, after only a brief exchange with one particular student of the Slobodka *yeshivah*, barely past his *bar-mitzvah*, he was sufficiently impressed to say, "Someday, half of the world will rest on this *bachur's* shoulders."

He was speaking of the very young Aharon Kotler.

It was clear even from youth that Reb Aharon was destined for greatness.

He was born in Sislov, a town in White Russia, in 5652 (1891), a descendant of the Pines family which had produced numerous great Torah scholars. His precocity in Torah studies was evident early on. By the age of five, he had memorized the *Chumash*, and by nine, he had already mastered the entire *Mesechte Kiddushin*. Two years later, he had learned the entire *Mesechte Kesuvos*, complete with every *Tosafos*.

Soon his fame had spread, and Rabbi Meir Simchah Hakohen of Dvinsk, the author of *Ohr Someach*, proclaimed him the greatest *ilui* (prodigy) of the past half century. Later, the Chafetz Chaim expressed his great admiration for the young scholar, and Rabbi Chaim Ozer Grodzenski remarked that "Reb Aharon is the Rabbi Akiva Eiger of his generation."

However, Reb Aharon himself never used his abilities as a springboard for gloating. He identified himself as only "Kotler" on the phone and insistently denied any claim to greatness. At a Chinuch Atzmai dinner, he was hailed as the leading *gaon* of the generation, while Reb Aharon tried desperately to stop the praise, tearfully exclaiming, "But that is not the *emes*!" After his passing, his widow noted that during their fifty years of marriage, he had never spoken about the achievements of his early years—nor, for that matter, about any aspect of his personal life at all.

Still honing his Torah skills, he joined Rabbi Reuven

Grozovsky and Rabbi Yaakov Kamenecki, two slightly older colleagues later to win renown in Torah circles, as students in a small *yeshivah* in Minsk. Their interaction there helped burnish their abilities. Finally, Reb Reuven, the oldest of the three, decided to transfer to a larger institution, and invited the others to do likewise.

Reb Yaakov was most agreeable, but there was some doubt as to whether young Aharon would follow suit. His father, Reb Shneur Zalman, had passed away, and his elder sister, who had strayed from Judaism and become a Communist, was pressing for Aharon to be sent to a secular institution; she foresaw a great career for him as a mathematician. She urged that he not "waste his life on these ancient studies" and sent him letters to that effect. However, Reb Reuven managed to suppress these letters, and Reb Aharon wound up joining his friends at the illustrious Slobodka Yeshivah. With typical humility, Reb Aharon later thanked Rabbi Grozovsky for doing so, since he had no way of knowing whether he could have withstood his sister's pressure.

The spirit of Slobodka was embodied by its guiding light Rabbi Nassan Tzvi Finkel, affectionately dubbed the "Alter of Slobodka." He instilled in his students an appreciation for the tenets of *Mussar*, and his own behavior personified the concepts he taught. He exuded a fatherly compassion for the *bnei yeshivah*. Tales abound of his pawning his possessions to provide them with money and giving them his own food and clothing to save them from the ravages of poverty. It was in Slobodka that Reb Aharon matured into a compassionate scholar and a genius who cared for his fellow man.

The Alter of Slobodka was most willing to share the fruits of his labors with the Jewish community at large. In 1897, when Rabbi Yaakov David Wilavsky (the Ridvaz) wished to have a *yeshivah* established in his town of Slutsk, the Alter came to his aid. He opened a branch of Slobodka in Slutsk and asked one of his foremost *talmidim*, Rabbi Isser Zalman

Meltzer, to serve as *rosh yeshivah*. The *yeshivah* thrived, and in 1911, Reb Aharon began delivering *shiurim* there. He eventually married Reb Isser Zalman's daughter and, as his son-in-law, became the *rosh yeshivah's* closest assistant.

Reb Aharon's wife Chana Perel was an outstanding personality in her own right. Her knowledge of *Tanach* was legendary, and her *tefillos* were inspirational in their purity. One who knew her said that she seemed to invite the presence of the *Shechinah*. The *yiras shamayim* she displayed in all her actions had a profound effect on their children Yosef Chaim Shneur (who later succeeded his father as *rosh yeshivah* in Lakewood) and Sarah.

World War I brought painful upheavals to Slutsk, as it did to other *yeshivos*. *Yeshivah* students found themselves caught in the crossfire and were forced to relocate time and time again. Then the situation worsened further. In October, 1917, Russia fell under Communist domination. The country's new masters dismissed religion as the "opium of the masses" and saw the Socialist ideals as humankind's salvation. Torah Judaism was considered a threat, to be diluted or smashed.

Under the new regime, Rabbi Meltzer was branded a subversive. He was arrested and sent to prison, charged with maintaining a religious institution. International outcries eventually led to his release, but the experience had proved how unwelcome Torah was in Russia. In 1925, Rabbi Meltzer decided to leave the country and accept an offer to lead the Yeshivas Etz Chaim in Eretz Yisrael.

Reb Aharon also felt the wrath of the Communist authorities. After an "invitation" to meet with them, he found it advisable to move the *yeshivah* to the city of Kletzk in Poland. There the *yeshivah* flourished, as Reb Aharon displayed the personal care for his *talmidim* that would become his hallmark in America as well. His *shiurim* were on a stratospheric level, and he argued his points with a fierce determination. After all, these were words of Torah, the holiest and most profound of all concepts, and they had to be probed with all the energy at one's disposal. However, he always made it abundantly clear that his sharp words were not a reflection of his feelings for the students. "If he argued with you," said a *talmid*, "it was a sign that he really valued your ideas and your opinions."

As a result, Kletzk drew students from throughout the world. From the United States came the young Gedaliah Schorr, a budding American *bachur* who would later become *rosh yeshivah* of Yeshivah Torah Vodaath. His American peers thought him odd for leaving the comfortable safety of the United States for a harsh life in a European *yeshivah*. Yet, Reb Gedaliah knew what he was doing. Under Reb Aharon's tutelage, he came to expand his already extensive knowledge and gained a keen appreciation for the European style of learning.

THE LONG ROUTE TO SAFETY

The first danger warnings penetrated the *koslei bais midrash* during the summer of 1939. Until then, in acknowledgment of their scholarly status, the Polish government had granted draft exemptions to the *yeshivah* students. Suddenly, however, the *bnei yeshivah* received army call-up notices. Reb Gedaliah Schorr was contacted by the American consulate and strongly advised to leave Poland and return to the United States. These emergency measures had a clear-cut cause: Nazi Germany was issuing grave threats that it would soon subjugate Poland.

Poland tried to gear up for the coming battle. However, its meager supply of outmoded armaments and its army dependent on nineteenth century war strategies were no match for the ultra-modern Nazi juggernaut. On September 1, 1939, Germany launched its crushing attack, using lightning-fast "blitzkrieg" tactics to defeat the enemy. Within two weeks, the conquest was all but complete. Polish Jewry was at the mercy of their sworn enemy.

Kletzk, swollen with refugees from nearby towns, braced for the Nazis' approach. On *Rosh Hashanah*, Kletzk's Jews fortified themselves with an unparalleled outpouring of prayer. Then, two days later, the first troops of occupation entered the city.

Fear gave way to amazement. These soldiers weren't German. They were Russian.

Now the features of the political jigsaw puzzle came into focus. The month before, Germany and Russia—until then, bitter ideological rivals—had suddenly signed a non-aggression treaty. With the invasion of Poland, it became clear that the pact had contained a secret deal. The countries would carve up the vanquished Poland. Germany would get the western part, and Russia would take over the east. Kletzk was therefore now in the Russian domain.

Some residents were jubilant. They were now free of the hated rule of the Polish government; they had been spared German domination, and they were safe.

Reb Aharon didn't share their euphoria. True, the Russians weren't the bloodthirsty beasts the Nazis were. But, as he had learned in Slutzk, Torah learning would become a target under the Communists. And if learning were impeded, Jewish life would eventually wither.

The day after *Sukkos*, Reb Aharon received a telegram from Reb Chaim Ozer Grodzenski, the sage of Vilna. Reb Chaim Ozer was convening an emergency conclave of *roshei yeshivah* from the area, and Reb Aharon's presence was urgently requested. On October 8, 1939, Reb Aharon left Kletzk—for what turned out to be the last time.

When the Torah leaders had gathered, Reb Chaim Ozer greeted them with stunning news. Vilna had long been a cause of contention between Poland and Lithuania. Each country claimed sovereignty over the city, and when the League of Nations granted Lithuania control of Vilna after World War I, Poland was outraged. It promptly sent troops into the region and forcibly wrested the city away.

However, Poland was now a defeated country, partly under Russian control. To the surprise of everyone, including the leaders of Lithuania, Russia now demanded that Poland return Vilna to Lithuania. That meant that, for the time being, Vilna was a political no-man's-land, unaligned with Russia or Poland, open to all. Steeped in tradition, and blessed with a vibrant Jewish community—and, most especially, with the benevolent guidance of Reb Chaim Ozer—Vilna was a natural refuge for Jews eager to escape the Russians. Now, through Divine Providence, these Jews could enter Vilna without undue difficulty.

"The *yeshivos*," declared Reb Chaim Ozer, "are welcome here, and we will do our best to provide for them as royally as possible. The learning must go on."

The *roshei yeshivah* accepted the generous offer. In their present locations, the *yeshivos* faced a very dubious future. But in Vilna, they could survive for a while, and hopefully find a means to leave Europe altogether.

On October 11, 1939, Reb Aharon dispatched a telegram to his family: "Leave Kletzk at once. You and the entire *yeshivah*. Come to Vilna immediately. Am awaiting you."

The message caused consternation among many of the *bnei yeshivah*. They, of course, revered their spiritual mentor, but they wondered why Reb Aharon was asking that they leave their families behind and undertake this strenuous journey. Was Vilna all that much safer than Kletzk? Hadn't some Jews already traveled there, only to return and decry the chaotic conditions in the city?

Nevertheless, they accepted the *rosh yeshivah's* word. After tearful farewells to their families and friends, the students and the Kotler family set out by horse-drawn wagons to

Baranowice, from where they would travel to Vilna by train.

At the station, they were greeted with the kind hospitality of the Baranowice Jews, and also by dire reports out of Vilna. Refugees were streaming there from all over Poland. Food was becoming scarce, and overcrowding was rife. Was the original plan still advisable? After consulting with Rebbetzin Kotler, some *bnei yeshivah* wired Reb Aharon on Friday: "Reports of major problems in Vilna. Should we still come?"

An hour before *Shabbos*, the reply arrived. "Yes! Immediately! Take the Friday night train!"

This last sentence stunned the *talmidim*. If Reb Aharon was urging them to transgress the sacred laws of *Shabbos*, the situation was grave indeed. After a quick but fervent *Kiddush* and a hasty *Shabbos* meal at the station, the Kletzk group boarded the train and arrived in Vilna on *Shabbos* morning. Having reached relative safety, they could not travel further and remained at the railroad terminal until sunset. There, they held a joyous reunion with Reb Aharon.

As he had promised, Reb Chaim Ozer saw to it that the *yeshivos* (which, besides Kletzk, included Mir, Bialystok, Radun, Kamenetz and Grodno, among others) had their needs met. Under his supervision, the Vilna Jewish communal council provided lodging, food and clothing for the *talmidim*, despite the general deprivations of wartime. Reb Chaim Ozer insisted that each *yeshivah* remain a separate entity, retaining its individual characteristics, and did everything to ensure that the learning would continue uninterrupted.

The political climate remained unstable. In October, 1939, Lithuania officially took control of Vilna, and with this, the influx of refugees flooding the city was curbed. A few months later, the situation deteriorated further. The Russians were back on the scene.

When he discovered that the *yeshivah* students had fled, the Communist commissar of Kletzk had rounded up the local citizens and addressed them: "When the Communists took over Slutsk, the members of your school escaped to Kletzk. Now, when we marched into Kletzk, they ran off to Vilna. They think they are safe. But what will they do when we take over Vilna?"

The commissar knew what he was talking about. Lithuania ruled Vilna for only a short while. Then, in June, 1940, the Russian media dramatically announced that Lithuania border troops had killed a Russian soldier. Using this incident as a pretext, Russia sent its tanks roaring across the border, and soon Lithuania was "voluntarily" asking for admission as a republic in the Soviet Union. By July, Vilna was in Russian hands, and the *yeshivos* were once again under Communist domination.

In the interval between September, 1939, and July, 1940, the *yeshivah* students maintained their *sedarim* of learning, while their spiritual mentors searched high and low for an escape route out of Europe. America and Eretz Yisrael were the popular choices for relocation, but each presented a serious problem. The United States refused to loosen its tight immigration quotas, and the British remained steadfast in barring Jewish entry to Palestine. The *yeshivah* contingent faced an uncertain future and suffered a grievous loss with the passing of Reb Chaim Ozer Grodzenski on August 9, 1940.

In February, 1940, Reb Aharon arranged for his two hundred and fifty Kletzk *talmidim* to move *en masse* to the town of Yanova, deeper in Lithuania. There they could study without the formidable distractions prevalent in a metropolis like Vilna. The townsfolk welcomed the young scholars with a hearty display of hospitality and arranged for comfortable living quarters for them.

Once the Russians intruded on the scene, though, this relatively quiet period ended. Government officials notified the *yeshivah* that it was too large for their approval. The crowd of students constituted a threat; their piety might rub off on the local populace, and that was intolerable. The *yeshivah* would have to subdivide, or else it would be disbanded entirely.

There was no choice but to split the *yeshivah* into three parts and to find a new home for each. One segment, headed by Rabbi Yosef Leib Nenedick, moved to Dusat, while another, composed of older *bachurim*, resettled in Dukst. Reb Aharon himself led the third group, which relocated to Salock, an isolated town near Dvinsk.

There the learning went on, but Reb Aharon was under no illusions. At any time, the Russians could close the *yeshivah* down. There had to be a way to escape their crushing rule, a way to secure passage to freedom. Reb Aharon intensified his one-man campaign to gain exit visas for his *talmidim*. He had raised funds in the United States in 1935, and he carried on an extensive correspondence with his contacts there, like Rabbi Israel Rosenberg, pleading for aid on his students' behalf.

"We wish that were possible," the reply came. "But getting permission for dozens of students to enter America is extremely hard. However, a few visas for distinguished individuals are being allowed, so there is a good chance of bringing you and your family over separately. Please consider this option seriously."

Reb Aharon, however, was most reluctant to accept it. How could he even think of leaving his students adrift? His heart and soul were intertwined with theirs; he placed their well-being above his own. Separating would be tantamount to tearing a mother away from her child. No, he would not depart without them.

Then reality made a nasty intrusion. One Friday, the *yeshivah's* secretary Reb Berel Starobin was seated at his rickety Hebrew typewriter, in the process of typing up Reb Aharon's Torah commentaries. Suddenly, the door burst open, and three burly brutes charged into the room. Reb Berel watched in horror as they began ransacking the office, apparently searching for incriminating evidence. Then they spied the typewriter.

"This is now government property," said one. He grabbed it and rushed outside.

"I have a message for your rabbi," another said. "Tell him to report to NKVD headquarters tonight at seven o'clock sharp. If he does not appear, we may have to come and escort him. He may not like that at all." He smiled smugly and then left.

Reb Berel relayed the man's words to Reb Aharon. The NKVD was the Russian secret police, and everyone knew that a summons to its headquarters was often equivalent to a death warrant. But such an invitation could not be declined.

Word of the incident quickly passed from one student to another. The *talmidim* were terrified, but Reb Aharon betrayed no fear. At night, he made *Kiddush* with his usual intense concentration and partook of the *Shabbos* meal. Then, with the anxious eyes of all the students fixed on him, he started towards the door.

"Can we come with you?" one *talmid* suddenly shouted, and others quickly echoed the plea. After all, if Reb Aharon arrived with a large entourage, the police might think twice of mistreating him.

Reb Aharon stopped and turned around. He was smiling. "I truly appreciate your concern. But I must go alone. The summons was for me only, and I cannot jeopardize the welfare of the entire *yeshivah*. Besides, if I came with a big contingent, they would think I was someone important and persecute me even more." He wished them well, and then he left, alone.

It was exactly seven o'clock when he arrived at his destination. "Are you Kotler?" a man barked.

Reb Aharon nodded.

"Then sit down," the man said.

He was joined by several NKVD agents, who stared at

Reb Aharon contemptuously. Finally, one held up a piece of paper. "Are these your writings?"

Reb Aharon recognized it as the page of Torah thoughts his secretary had been typing, and he said so. Was this their proof of his subversion?

"Why do you waste your time with this religious nonsense?" the man went on. "Don't you have anything better to do with your time?"

"Excuse me, but these religious writings are very dear to me," Reb Aharon replied in a controlled voice. "I take my religious beliefs very seriously, and I'm sure I needn't remind you that according to the Russian Constitution everyone is entitled to freedom of religion."

The NKVD agents looked at each other.

Another man tried a different approach. "You seem to be a very powerful individual. After all, all those young men in Salock seem to be studying under you."

"There are no young men with me now, are there?" said Reb Aharon.

"But aren't they your rabbinical students?"

"I don't know. Maybe."

"And don't they take their orders from you?"

"I never give orders to anyone. This is a free country, isn't it? Everyone does what he wishes."

The men were growing frustrated. "How about the coming elections for the Supreme Soviet. Are you planning to vote?"

"Certainly."

"And whom will you choose? A Jewish candidate?"

"I will vote for whomever the government advises. I assume the government will make the correct decision. Don't you agree?"

The questioner shrugged and looked at his colleagues. Then he spoke again. "All right, you can go. For now. But we may have another chat soon."

Very soon Reb Aharon was back within the reassuring walls of the *yeshivah*.

"*Baruch Hashem*, they let me go," he told the relieved students. But he knew his reprieve might be only temporary. The government could arrest him again at any time. He was marked for harassment, and his days with the *yeshivah* were undoubtedly numbered.

Reb Aharon began rethinking his alternatives.

If he remained in Russia, there was little he could do. But if he was in America, he might accomplish something positive. Once in the free world, there was the chance that he might work effectively to bring his beloved students to safety.

This was the course he decided on. He would go to America—not because it promised to provide personal safety, but because it offered the chance of saving his entire student body.

In early 1941, he, his wife and daughter took their leave of the *yeshivah*. (His son Shneur had been one of those fortunate to receive a visa for Eretz Yisrael, where his grandfather Rabbi Isser Zalman Meltzer lived; he had already reached the Holy Land.) A large crowd of rabbis, *baalei batim* and, of course, *yeshivah* students saw him off on the long journey.

The trip was not an easy one. An American official named Laurence Steinhardt had dispatched visas for the family, and Reb Aharon was told to go to Moscow to pick them up. However, when he arrived at the American embassy in Moscow, he found that a bureaucratic foul-up had occurred and no one knew anything about visas for the Kotlers. Refugees had to conclude their business in Moscow within twenty-four hours before being made to leave the city. Reb Aharon wired Elimelech Tress in New York to see what could be done.

Tress sprang into action, and with the approval of Rabbi Shlomo Heiman and Rabbi Gedaliah Schorr, travelled to Washington that day, which was *Shabbos*. By chance, he came upon Undersecretary of State Breckenridge Long, who agreed to help. But when they tried to reach Reb Aharon, they found that his twenty-four-hour waiting period had expired, and that he had already left Moscow.

Reb Aharon's *bitachon* carried him through the crisis, and he decided to take a chance. He and his family left without the visas and boarded a train on the Trans-Siberian Railroad that would carry them across Russia. At the end of their journey, in the Pacific coast port of Vladivostok, they noticed a Russian official staring straight at them. Would he discover that they lacked the necessary papers?

The official was suddenly distracted and looked away. The Kotlers were free to go.

There were other close calls, other officials who almost caught them, but each time the danger passed. After the train trip, the Kotlers made their way to Kobe, Japan, which they reached by February, 1941. From there, they were off to America.

On April 10, 1941, the day before *Pesach*, Reb Aharon arrived in Los Angeles. Days later, during *Chol Hamoed*, he left by train for New York. A new era was beginning—for Reb Aharon, and for American Jewry.

"ACT NOW!"

Reb Aharon's comments at Penn Station were only the opening shot in the vigilant campaign he would now be waging. Immediately afterwards, he joined Rabbi Silver at a gathering of the Agudath Harabbanim, where he was asked to speak. Elaborating on his earlier remarks, he came right to the point.

"*Rabbosai*, what we are experiencing now is destruction of a magnitude not seen since the *Churban Bais Hamikdash*," he told his colleagues. "The troubles of the past pale in comparison with those we are seeing now.

"Our Torah scholars in Europe, uprooted from their homes and facing frightening conditions, still remain at their posts with an awesome sense of responsibility. They cope with despair and a bleak future, but they stand determined, encouraged by the hope that assistance and salvation will come.

"We have to act now! We have to send them financial support! Above all, we have to save these precious jewels of our people. The guarantee of our continued existence lies in the rescue of our Torah scholars.

"And it is up to us to take the lead. This land, the United States of America, is the only one that can really help those trapped in Europe. We have the wealth and the resources, and we must use them. We must save the scholars and build new homes for Torah on these shores. Let us remember the words of the saintly Rav Chaim of Volozhin a century ago: 'Torah is destined to wander from place to place and find many different homes before the coming of the *Mashiach*—and the last stop along this journey will be America!'

"Therefore, those of us who live here in relative peace and tranquility must give up some of our comforts during this time of duress and tragedy. We must give unstintingly of our time, our energies and our wealth to come to the aid of our beleaguered brothers. We must raise money to help them survive until we win their freedom. If we fail now, we will lose this golden opportunity forever.

"I issue this call to all those to whom Torah and the Jewish people are dear. This undertaking must transcend any political considerations. Time is short. We cannot carry on with a business-as-usual attitude. Those who delay in this holy work are actually shedding blood."

Reb Aharon's words had an impact. With his arrival in the United States, American Jewish rescue work took on a new sense of urgency and a more potent course.

Since its founding in 1939, Vaad Hatzalah had been

conducting outstanding work on behalf of the endangered Torah scholars in Europe. (See Chapter Two in this volume.) An independent organization under the direction of sages like Rabbi Eliezer Silver, aided by the efforts of Elimelech Tress and his young Zeirei workers, it had already helped secure the rescue of such Torah leaders as Rabbi Avraham Kalmanowitz (who had immediately plunged into *hatzalah* efforts himself). Now, with Rabbi Kotler (and soon after, his old colleague Rabbi Reuven Grozovsky) joining the helm of the Vaad and bolstering it with their remarkable wisdom and boundless energy, its work became more focused and efficient.

One of Reb Aharon's primary goals was making sure the Vaad had a unified stand.

"This is a time of unparalleled crisis," he reminded his colleagues. "How can we squander our energies with petty bickering and senseless political rivalries? When it comes to saving lives, we are a family. We have to act together, as one!"

THOSE LEFT BEHIND

Though he worked relentlessly to save any Jew he could, Reb Aharon was especially concerned with rescuing the Torah scholars still in danger. The haunting image of the *yeshivah* students he had left behind never escaped him. He always bore in mind that he had come to America for one reason only—to use his influence to bring them over as soon as possible.

It quickly became apparent, though, that he faced an uphill battle. By now, the Russians had closed their borders tight. In fact, Reb Aharon had been one of the last to flee the country before the doors had slammed shut.

On June 6, 1941, the members of the Kletzk Yeshivah still in Salock were ordered to report to the office of the local constable. There, they were confronted with a question: Did they wish to remain in the Soviet Union and apply for Soviet citizenship? Or did they want to leave Salock and return to their home towns?

The students knew that the question was a loaded one. If they rejected Soviet citizenship, they would likely be dealt with severely. On the other hand, they felt only antipathy for the Soviet system. They could never pledge allegiance to a government that sought to squelch the free practice of religion. No matter what the Russians did to them, it could hardly be worse than living under constant Communist surveillance.

As a result, most of the *talmidim* opted against Soviet citizenship. The Communists' reaction came swiftly enough.

One week later, a gang of Russian rowdies gathered in front of the *yeshivah's* quarters. "We've been sent here by the authorities. We have to escort you to the buses."

"Why do we need buses?" asked a *talmid*.

"Don't you know? You're setting off on a nice, long journey to a very friendly place. It's called Siberia."

So much for those who couldn't fit neatly into "Stalin's Paradise."

The students of Kletzk were among the contingents of many *yeshivos* sent off to the Soviet wasteland, along with hundreds of thousands of their fellow Jews. It seemed a brutal, numbing fate, the worst of all possible punishments. The *yeshivah* students were relieved that a few of their number had chosen to accept Soviet citizenship. They, at least, would remain behind in safety. Little did they know what the future bore.

On June 22, 1941, only nine days after the roundup, the Germans launched a major surprise attack on Russia. Hitler had stabbed his supposed ally in the back, with astoundingly successful results. The Nazi march pressed forward with ease, as the Russian armies melted away.

Soon the Nazis came upon Salock, as well as the neighboring villages. They didn't hesitate, having by now nearly perfected their methods. The Jews of the area were rounded up and told to dig their own graves. Then they were shot to death.

The same fate befell those in Kletzk. On October 30, 1941, four thousand of the city's Jews were ordered to stand in front of an enormous ditch. The command was given, and the machine guns blazed. Soon the ditch had become a mass burial plot. The eight hundred and fifty Jews who did not die in this manner were herded into a ghetto, and for nine months went through untold suffering. Then, on July 19, 1942, the ghetto was liquidated, and almost all of these Jews died, too.

The escape to Vilna had proved a lifesaver. If the students had remained in Kletzk, they would almost certainly have shared the fate of the families they had left behind.

At the time, though, they had no way of knowing this; and the grueling existence in Siberia seemed as harsh a penalty as was imaginable. Braving the frigid weather, forced to work in the dreadful labor camps, taunted mercilessly by their captors, the students prayed for help. (Later, the Russians would transfer many of these Siberian laborers to Central Asia, where they suffered from the intense heat instead.)

Their *rosh yeshivah* tried to provide the assistance they craved. He joined the other Vaad Hatzalah activists in raising funds for the deprived *talmidim*, visiting one Jewish community after another in a never-ending search for assistance.

Then, under the Vaad's auspices, he began sending food packages to Jews being held in Siberia and other Russian sites. The parcels contained rare items, like saccharine, which could be bartered for life-sustaining food and clothing. However, the packages would take time to arrive.

Therefore, at Reb Aharon's insistence, the Vaad began wiring money directly to the Jews in Siberia. This met with fierce opposition. Secular critics charged that, due to the rate of monetary exchange, over eighty percent of the money would be lost through the transference. They also questioned whether the funds or the packages would ever wind up in the right hands. It all seemed like a waste of resources and effort.

Reb Aharon vehemently disagreed. "We must do our part to help our brothers and sisters," he insisted. "True, our efforts won't always succeed. But that is not the point. What is important is that we try. We have to play our role to the fullest. The rest is up to Hashem. If He sees that we are doing the very best we can, then maybe He will bless our work and help us succeed.

"Therefore, this work has to go on. Even if only a minute portion of the money or a few of the packages arrive at their destination, and even if only one or two Jews are helped by it, we must continue. That is our task."

Eventually, it came to light that the success rate had been far higher than anticipated. Numerous packages and much of the money did reach the suffering Jews, and often made the difference between starving and surviving. Alter Pekier, a *talmid* of the Kletzk Yeshivah, received one of the packages after a tormenting period in a Siberian labor camp. The contents helped him enormously in his daily struggle for survival, but they also meant more. They showed him that his *rosh yeshivah*, his guiding shepherd, hadn't forgotten him and was still tenderly tending his sheep wherever they wandered.

CONTACTS WITH CLOUT

Aid was needed in other quarters, too. Over five hundred Torah scholars, including virtually the entire Mirrer Yeshivah student body (as well as eighty *rabbanim*, their families and students of other *yeshivos*) had managed to escape from Russia and had arrived in Japan. However, they were then unable to proceed to freedom, and the Japanese had transferred them to Shanghai. (See Volume I, Chapter 2.) There they pursued their Torah studies, while continuing to search for an escape route to the free world. However, when war broke out between Japan and the United States, all direct contact with Torah scholars was lost. American aid to the Shanghai Jewish refugee community, which had been provided mainly by the Joint Distribution Committee, was now forbidden. Unless the Vaad found an alternate aid route, the refugees in Shanghai would slowly wither away. But would the American government allow such a route?

The ultimate solution, though, was not sending packages or money to the European Jews. The best way of ensuring the Jews' safety was to bring them to America.

Yet, the immigration quotas remained securely in place. The government wouldn't bend an inch.

Wasn't there any way of making the government more responsive to the crisis? Couldn't the stone hearts of the bureaucrats be melted at all?

The time was at hand to expand the Vaad's contacts with United States officials.

Almost as soon as he had set foot in the U.S., Rabbi Kotler had sought to meet with no less than Franklin D. Roosevelt, the President himself. He was confident that if he could just convey the anguish of the suffering Jews to the President, Roosevelt would view their plight more sympathetically. Unfortunately, Roosevelt's time was limited, and so was his interest in Jewish woes. The Jews he did agree to see, like Stephen Wise, were so enamored of the President that they failed to see his faults.

Yet, even if he couldn't gain access to the President, Reb Aharon could still reach out to the upper echelons of government. With very limited resources, he began contacting Senators and Congressmen, alerting them to the Jews' plight and asking for help. That Reb Aharon knew almost no English didn't deter him. He simply had Vaad workers who were fluent in English speak for him, and he told them what to say.

Soon, a number of powerful legislators had come to support the Vaad's initiatives. They included Senator Robert Taft, a long-time acquaintance of Rabbi Silver, and Congressman Emanuel Celler, who was powerfully influenced by Rabbi Kalmanowitz's pleas. However, the Vaad leaders felt it imperative to be heard in the Administration. If they couldn't meet Roosevelt, perhaps they could see one of his top aides. But whom?

After much deliberation, the Vaad leaders decided on Treasury Secretary Henry Morgenthau. He had access to Roosevelt, and he was a Jew—although hardly an observant one. In fact, he had exhibited little kinship with his fellow Jews. Still, it was worth a try.

Through the intercession of Rabbi Baruch Korff, a young Boston clergyman, a small group, which included Rabbi Kotler and Rabbi Kalmanowitz, was given an appointment to meet with the Treasury Secretary in his Washington office in 1942. Initially, they found Morgenthau quite reserved and guarded. These European Rabbis were obviously an alien sight to him. But as he listened to their arguments, the chill slowly began to dissipate. Something seemed to penetrate to his conscience and reawaken his faint sense of Jewishness.

"Please speak to the President," they pleaded. "Please ask him to change his policy and save the Jews of Europe before it is too late."

The delegates waited, fully expecting him to brush them off. Instead, Morgenthau sat quietly, pondering their words. Then he picked up the phone. "Get me Secretary of State Hull, please."

"Mr. Hull is at a meeting, Mr. Secretary," he was told. "He can't be disturbed."

"Tell him it is imperative that he call me back. I want him to arrange a meeting between me and the President about the murder of the Jews of Europe by the Nazis. I will be waiting here right by the phone, and I expect an answer shortly."

Soon Hull's assistant Sumner Welles called back. "Mr. Hull has received your message, and he asked me to tell you that he doesn't think this is the right time to bring up the Jewish issue. The situation is too delicate right now."

Suddenly, Morgenthau's ire flamed. "You tell Mr. Hull that this is the first time in all my years in government service that I ever asked to meet with the President on a personal matter—a matter that concerns my people. If I am turned down on this, there may be very negative consequences."

The delegation members were astounded. They had never expected Morgenthau to be so assertive about the issue. It heartened them greatly.

They waited some more, until the phone rang again. "Mr. Hull says that your meeting has been approved."

Morgenthau's encounter with the President did not bring immediate salvation to Europe's Jews. However, the episode marked a turning point in Morgenthau's emergence as a sympathetic advocate of the Vaad's cause. They would come to call on him again and again, and he eventually helped them work out a legal way of sending aid to the Shanghai Jews through the Sternbuchs in neutral Switzerland.

Sadly, the need for this intervention became more and more evident as the war progressed and the news grew worse. By the fall of 1942, shocking reports, relayed by the Sternbuchs and Gerhard Riegner in Switzerland, had confirmed the unbelievable. Jews were being massacred in unprecedented numbers. (See Volume I, Chapter 5.) Millions had already been murdered, and millions more would follow unless something was done—immediately!

The leaders of the Vaad reacted as if their house was ablaze. They persuaded the powerful Stephen Wise to call a meeting of Jewish leaders of all stripes in order to demand action on behalf of European Jewry. The Vaad was most willing to work with anyone who had the influence and resources to save Jewish lives, no matter what his beliefs.

When he was criticized for dealing with the secular, anti-religious Wise, Reb Aharon didn't change his approach. "I would work with the Pope himself," he shot back, "if it would help save the fingernail of even one Jewish child."

However, Wise didn't share the Orthodox Jews' sense of urgency. He submitted the reports to the State Department, which advised total silence about the issue while they verified its authenticity. This went on for months. Meanwhile, the murders in Europe continued. Nevertheless, Wise used his authority to order all Jewish groups to remain quiet about the report. Orthodox Jewish leaders were forced to agree but demanded in return that a new committee be formed to meet with the President about rescuing Jews.

Finally, the State Department announced their findings. The reports were accurate. Millions of Jews had indeed gone to their deaths. Roosevelt agreed to meet with a small delegation of the new Jewish committee, but only once. Nothing came of the get-together, and Wise deflected all criticism of his idol, the President.

The leaders of the Vaad came to a regretful conclusion. They would get nowhere by letting other groups set the agenda. From now on, they would have to take the initiative. The Vaad would expand its efforts and be concerned with the rescue of *all* Jews, from Torah scholars to non-believers.

Fundraising went into high gear, and by 1944, with the collection drives of Zeirei Agudath Israel leading the way, the Vaad's budget had skyrocketed tenfold to over a million dollars. Joint planning with the activist Revisionist Zionists, headed by Peter Bergson, led to a Rabbis' March on Washington in October 1943. (See Chapter Two in this volume.) This venture helped pave the way, in January, 1944, for the formation of the War Refugee Board, the only government agency devoted to rescue work. Rabbi Kotler played a significant behind-the-scenes role in smoothing over political differences among Jewish groups calling for the Board's creation.

A SHARP RETORT

Another initiative that drew the Vaad's active support was the Musy Mission of 1944-5. (See Volume I, Chapter 5.) This effort, promoted by the Sternbuchs in Switzerland, was a last-ditch attempt to save over half a million Jews through negotiations with Nazi leaders like Heinrich Himmler. Himmler, who realized the war was going badly for the Nazis, stated his willingness to release the remaining Jews (whose numbers were down to only three hundred thousand by February, 1945) in exchange for five million dollars. Musy, a former president of Switzerland, managed to have that sum reduced to a million and a quarter dollars, plus favorable media publicity for the Nazis. As a sign of good faith, after a first payment, Himmler had released some thirteen hundred Jews via the so-called "Kastner train."

The deal seemed a miraculous opportunity, but major problems abounded. Raising a million dollars on short notice was an enormously formidable task for the Vaad. The affluent Joint Distribution Committee could certainly provide it but would almost certainly refuse; they called such payments ransom and rejected all illegal deals with the enemy. Nevertheless, a Vaad delegation, led by Rabbi Kotler and Rabbi Kalmanowitz and the indefatigable lay leader Irving Bunim, met with Joint president Moe Leavitt to discuss a loan.

Leavitt was testy. "How can you possibly ask us to deal with those murderers? Don't you know that they'll just use the money to continue the war?"

"But they've kept their part of the deal so far," Rabbi Kotler reminded him. "They said they would release Jews from the camps, and they did. How can we let this opportunity pass us by?"

"Do you think those they let out of the camps were really Jews? Many of them weren't religious Jews. They were converts, that's who they were!"

Reb Aharon had no way of knowing if this was true, but even if it was, it didn't matter to him. "Who knows why they converted? Maybe they were forced into it. Even so, they are still Jews, and they deserved to be helped!"

Leavitt was growing impatient. "Who are you to decide what we should do?" he fumed. "We are the major relief organization in the Jewish world, the department store. You are only a pushcart."

Though he was angered, Irving Bunim kept his composure. "What are we arguing like this for? The Jews in Europe certainly need the Joint, but they also need the Vaad. We have different priorities; we get things done in different ways. You always follow the law to the letter, but when it comes to rescue work, we save lives and think of the consequences later.

"Think of it this way. If your son were a soldier, and he was wounded in battle before your eyes, would you just stand by and wait for a doctor to come and treat him? Or would you immediately rush over to see how you could help? Well, that's the way we see things. You want to wait till the war ends before you can help the Jews in Europe. But to us, every Jew is a member of the family, and we want to assist him right away, in any way possible."

Finally, after Bunim threatened to publicize the Joint's lack of cooperation, Leavitt agreed to sponsor the loan, but on one condition. The American government had to issue a license transferring the money overseas.

However, this was hardly a simple matter. The government was adamantly opposed to any transactions with Germany before total victory was achieved. Nevertheless, the members of the Vaad were determined to proceed with every resource at their disposal. The lives of hundreds of thousands of Jews could not be dismissed with the words, "It can't be done."

After extensive deliberations, the Vaad leaders decided

to make their case before the President himself. Once again, though, they were informed that Roosevelt was unavailable. Instead, they were referred to Treasury Secretary Morgenthau.

They had won Morgenthau's sympathy before, but this was a different matter. "Paying ransom to the Nazis is out of the question," was his snap reaction. "The American public would never accept such a thing. There is no way I can get the President to approve it. If I'd ask him, I'd just be putting my job on the line. And if I were fired, what good would I be?"

Reb Aharon, who knew little English, normally required someone else to translate for him. In this case, it was Irving Bunim. However, Morgenthau's tone of voice was sign enough of his response. Even before Bunim could begin translating, Reb Aharon had a reply for Morgenthau. Others might be intimidated by the man's high position, but Reb Aharon saw before him only the Jews who had just been doomed.

Turning to Bunim, he said, "You tell him the following. If he cannot help save the lives of his fellow Jews, then his high-ranking job is worth nothing! One Jewish life is worth more than all the top-level jobs in Washington! Hashem put him in his position so he could help his people, and if he doesn't take advantage of it, then he is nobody!"

The words were uttered in Yiddish, but their angry intent was obvious. Still, Bunim, fearful of Morgenthau's reaction, was hesitant to translate them. He began mumbling a benign version of Rabbi Kotler's remarks, and the Secretary looked relieved. But Reb Aharon understood that he had not been quoted correctly.

"No," he insisted. "Tell him exactly what I said!"

This time, Bunim did so. Nervously, he anticipated Morgenthau's outraged response.

Instead, the Secretary put his head in his hands and remained silent for what seemed an eternity. Finally, he looked straight at Rabbi Kotler.

"Tell the Rabbi that first and foremost, I am a Jew," he

said to Bunim. "And tell him that I am willing to give up my life—not just my position—for my fellow Jews."

Eventually, after some difficult legal wrangling, Morgenthau won approval for the license, and the loan was transferred. (This helped lead to the release of twelve hundred Jews from Thereisenstadt.) Unfortunately, the Musy Mission ran aground when the favorable media coverage demanded by Himmler came to Hitler's attention. The furious Fuhrer immediately scuttled the deal, and the killings went on. However, the contacts established by Musy helped spare the lives of thousands of Jews in the concentration camps who might otherwise have been killed before the Allies liberated them.

QUALITIES OF LEADERSHIP

Guiding Reb Aharon's rescue work, of course, were the Torah principles that served as beacons for all his endeavors throughout his life.

He often cited the example of Mordechai, who was chosen by Hashem to be instrumental in effecting the hidden miracles of *Purim*. Why had he merited this distinction? Because, unlike the other Jews of his generation, he was untainted by a desire for personal gain. His fellow Jews of Shushan had taken part in King Achashverosh's feast and had enjoyed that illicit affair, drinking with abandon from vessels captured from the *Bais Hamikdash*. Not Mordechai. He remained pure, and it was he who was, therefore, selected to do the work of Hashem.

Reb Aharon looked for this integrity in others and demanded it of himself.

Thus, the suffering of his fellow Jews in Europe was very real to him. They were his family; while they lived in pain, so did he.

As a rule, Reb Aharon subsisted on very little. The furnishings in his simple home were the barest minimum. However, during the war, he voluntarily suffered even greater privations. As an act of empathy with the suffering Jews of Europe, his *rebbetzin* made a point of denying herself tea, her favorite drink, throughout the war years, except on *Shabbos*. And visitors to his home noticed a pervasive atmosphere of mourning that lasted until the Nazis' defeat.

Reb Aharon avoided any hint of personal benefit derived through his rescue work. Once he and Irving Bunim were in the process of forwarding funds they had raised towards the rescue of Jews stranded in Shanghai. Bunim was about to write out a check for this purpose, when Reb Aharon suddenly stopped him.

"Here," said the sage, holding out money of his own. "Add this to the total."

"But I think we have enough," Bunim said. "The *rosh yeshivah* doesn't have to use his own personal funds."

"Yes, I do. You see, I think there is a young woman in that group who may soon become my daughter-in-law. I don't want it said that I benefitted in any way from the *tzedakah* donated by the public on behalf of the refugees."

Yet, at the same time, he was willing to accept any exertion and suffer any indignity in his crusade to raise funds for others, whether in the realm of *hatzalah* or in support of other Torah causes.

On numerous occasions, he made arduous trips to wealthy individuals seeking a generous contribution—only to be rewarded with a pittance. One such time, Irving Bunim, who had accompanied him, could not contain his anger. "What galls me is that the *rosh yeshivah* had to give up his invaluable time and energy, only to be sent away with a few pennies from someone who could have given so much more!"

Reb Aharon quickly calmed him. "Don't blame the man. If anything, pity him. He might be so worried about the ups and downs of his business that he can't see the wisdom of investing in Torah. And as for me, don't worry. I accept any suffering that comes of working for Torah causes. If it is done for the sake of Hashem, then any indignity is worth it."

After another such instance, he explained that disappointments were to be expected. "*Chazal* tell us that we were deprived of the second *Bais Hamikdash* and condemned to *galus* because we did not treat our fellow Jews properly. As a teacher of Torah, I have had the occasion to teach many students. Who knows? Undoubtedly, I have given cutting answers to some of the *talmidim* and upset them. Now I am forced to pay for my mistakes by wandering from place to place seeking funds. It is decreed from Heaven, and I accept it fully."

However, no matter how inappropriately Reb Aharon himself might have been treated, he was always mindful of the feelings of others. He may have been impatient in his dealings with languid bureaucrats during his rescue work and sharp in making his points during Torah discussions, but on a personal level, he was caring and considerate.

The members of his family were, of course, dear to him. One time, he was being driven to an important meeting, when he suddenly asked the driver to stop and turn back. The driver naturally assumed that Reb Aharon had accidentally left behind some significant item. He accompanied the *rosh yeshivah* back to his home and discovered the reason for the abrupt return.

Reb Aharon had neglected to say goodbye to his *rebbetzin*.

Yet, his "loved ones" included not just his relations. As his *rebbetzin* was fond of saying, "Yes, he loves his grandchildren—almost as much as he loves his *talmidim*."

His students enjoyed a special place in his heart. They represented the process of perpetuating the Torah heritage. Reb Aharon was not one to lock himself away in his study, appearing before them only in a lecture room. Rather, on

Shabbos he would join them in the *yeshivah* dining room, exchanging Torah thoughts with them and sharing their lives.

His *talmidim* were eager to serve him, but he never treated them as anything but equals in the mission at hand.

On one lengthy trip, he took very little by way of refreshments, only an orange, which he ate after carefully putting the peel in a paper bag, so as not to litter. The student accompanying him offered to take the bag off the *rosh yeshivah's* hands. Reb Aharon vigorously refused.

"You are a Torah student—a prince among men—not a servant to carry around my refuse."

After an exhausting fundraising excursion, Reb Aharon returned home late at night. Suddenly, the student accompanying him heard him exclaim, "Oh! I have been so preoccupied today that I've neglected my Torah studies!"

The student was somewhat perplexed, recalling how Reb Aharon had engaged him in lengthy Torah conversations throughout the trip, when not immersed in the *sefer* that never left his hands. Nevertheless, Reb Aharon immediately opened a *Gemara* and delved into an abstruse *sugya*.

"But I've prepared something for you to eat," the *rebbetzin* said. "It's been a long day. You must be famished."

"I'm not hungry, but please give it to him," Reb Aharon replied, indicating the student. "After all, he's done the really tiring work, driving all day. He truly deserves a feast."

The student then dined under the concerned eyes of the *rosh yeshivah* and the *rebbetzin*.

The next day, he received a phone call. It was Reb Aharon, wanting to know if the young man was in good health after the arduous trip and worried that he had not sufficiently thanked him for his services.

Among those receiving Reb Aharon's supreme gratitude were those who had aided the rescue drive or the campaigns for Torah causes.

It was well past midnight, many years later, when a

student at the Lakewood Yeshivah was awakened by a knock at his dormitory door. Rather disturbed by the late-night intrusion, he was about to berate his visitor, when he noticed that it was none other than Reb Aharon himself.

"Could you do me a great favor?" the *rosh yeshivah* said. "Perhaps you could wake up a few other *talmidim* and arrange for a *minyan* right away in the *bais midrash*? I've just received word that Rabbi Emanuel Lederman of Denver is very ill. We have to say *Tehillim* for him."

The student was agreeable, but had a suggestion. "The other *bachurim* might be upset if I wake them up at this hour. It will be much easier assembling a *minyan* tomorrow morning, if the *rosh yeshivah* doesn't mind waiting a bit."

"But you don't understand," Reb Aharon replied. "You may not have heard of Rabbi Lederman, but I will never forget him. When the Vaad Hatzalah was trying to raise funds to ransom Jews from the concentration camps, I sent telegrams to rabbis around the country, asking for help. Rabbi Lederman was the very first to respond. His contribution came in at three o'clock in the morning! So it is only right that we return the favor and say *Tehillim* for him immediately, even if it is the middle of the night. I'm sorry to inconvenience everyone, but it's a matter of *hakaras hatov* (expressing gratitude)."

Likewise, Reb Aharon insisted on attending a wedding in Long Island, even though it entailed a two-hour trip on a suffocatingly hot summer day. Some tried to dissuade him, saying that the trip would be too onerous. Reb Aharon brushed them aside.

"The bride's father asked me to attend, and I cannot disappoint him," he explained. "After all, he has done much to support Torah, and he deserves our everlasting gratitude. Going to his *simchah* is the least I can do for him."

In the end, though, his respect was conveyed on a universal basis for all humankind.

He thought nothing of running after a beggar collecting

alms and being overjoyed at catching up with him and making a large donation. Why? "Recently he asked me for a donation, and I didn't have any money on me. I just happened to see him again in the street, and this gave me the chance to finally help him out—and to make up for last time by giving him double."

Likewise, someone noticed him giving *tzedakah* to a poor person when entering a *shul*—and giving to the same person again upon leaving. Why was this necessary? "Not everyone knew that I donated to the man the first time. Therefore, if they saw me pass him by on the way out without giving, they might have thought that his cause wasn't worthwhile. How could I let that happen?"

Once the *rosh yeshivah* was being chauffeured back from a nocturnal meeting, and the driver was eager to speed the journey. They came to a toll booth. Suddenly, Reb Aharon peered up. "Excuse me, but where are you going?"

"I'm taking the automatic toll lane, if that's all right, *rebbe*," the driver explained. "That way I can just throw a token into the machine. It will help us get off the highway a bit more quickly, so the *rosh yeshivah* can return to the *yeshivah* sooner."

"If you don't mind, could you use the other lane, the one with the attendant?" Reb Aharon said. "I know it might take longer. Nevertheless, I don't want the man at the booth to think that we passed him by in favor of a machine."

To him, it was a clear-cut matter of *kavod habriyos*.

A CHERISHED DISCIPLE

Throughout his lifetime, Reb Aharon inspired countless followers of all ages. One whose association with Reb Aharon proved especially rewarding was Irving Bunim. The fruits of their symbiotic relationship blanketed *Klal Yisrael* with numerous blessings.

Bunim was born in Volozhin, in Lithuania, but he moved to New York with his family at the age of nine. He established himself as a typical, successful American businessman, and then began devoting much of his prodigious energies to *klal* work, especially on behalf of the Young Israel movement. He had been one of the original lay leaders of Vaad Hatzalah and was present when Reb Aharon made his appearance at Penn Station in April, 1941. Bunim was so taken with Reb Aharon's words at that first encounter that he immediately made *hatzalah* work his top priority. Whenever Reb Aharon called, Bunim jumped to respond—and considered it the ultimate privilege.

Though Bunim was a proudly observant Jew and a *lamdan* in his own right, he always claimed that he learned more from observing Reb Aharon than from any other source. He found in the *rosh yeshivah* a leader of astute counsel and a keen judge of human nature, someone with a firm grasp of how to best deal with even the most worldly public figures.

Bunim accompanied Reb Aharon on a number of trips to Washington, where they became familiar Congressional and White House lobbyists in the cause of rescue.

One such meeting, in 1944, coincided with *Asarah Beteves*, a fast day. They had arrived in Washington the day before, and Reb Aharon had arranged to stay at the home of a friend, while Bunim had insisted on registering at a hotel. When they met the next morning, Bunim noticed that Reb Aharon was carrying a bag filled with rolls and hot coffee.

"What are these for, *rebbe*?" asked Bunim, thinking that in the flurry of activity Reb Aharon had perhaps forgotten the date.

Not at all. "It will be a difficult day, and you will need all the energy you can muster," Reb Aharon told Bunim. "Since you will be involved in helping to save lives, and since this fast is only based on Rabbinical decree, it is my opinion that you can eat."

Bunim demurred. "I feel fine, *Rebbe*. I think I can make it without the food."

"*Nu*, if you feel good, then fast."

The meetings went well, but they were long and, as Reb Aharon had predicted, took their toll. By the time they were over in the afternoon, Bunim was exhausted. As the two took their seats in the train for their return journey, Bunim noticed Reb Aharon still holding the bag of food. "*Now*, I feel I could really eat a feast," he grinned.

Reb Aharon returned the smile. "Our mission is over," he reminded Bunim, "so now you could fast."

That same year, as the Allies closed in on the battered German armies, Reb Aharon received word from the Sternbuchs that the Nazis were planning to separate Jewish prisoners of war from other captured Allied soldiers and deal with them individually—a very ominous development.

Reb Aharon did not get bogged down in indecision. Immediately, he called Irving Bunim and told him, "Get ready to leave for Washington first thing in the morning!"

The next morning, Bunim came to Reb Aharon's residence, only to find the *rosh yeshivah* laid low by illness and hardly able to walk. "*Rebbe*, you're in no condition to make the trip. I'll go by myself."

Reb Aharon wouldn't hear of it. He insisted on coming along, since there was the possibility of finally meeting with President Roosevelt.

On the train, Bunim wrote up the draft of a memorandum to be submitted to government officials, calling for the Allies to protest vigorously the latest Nazi outrage. When it was finished, he began reading it to Reb Aharon for his approval.

"It is a sad story that after twenty centuries of oppression, murder and pogroms, you will allow the Nazis to proceed with the destruction of the Jewish prisoners of war."

"Wait!" Reb Aharon suddenly shouted. "Leave that part out!"

Bunim was astounded. "But that was just the beginning, and it stated the obvious. What could be wrong with it?"

"Think for a moment," Reb Aharon explained. "Suppose a gentile official reads that, someone who is not particularly a friend of the Jews. When he comes on those words, he'll say to himself, 'The Jews have been persecuted for two thousand years already! So what's wrong if the Germans persecute them a little longer? It won't make much difference.'"

Bunim saw the wisdom of Reb Aharon's thinking and quickly altered the text. Then, when he had finished his revisions, Reb Aharon had another suggestion. Perhaps Roosevelt would not be the best choice to receive the memorandum. It would probably get lost amidst all his other papers; and besides, he had never indicated a deep-rooted sympathy for the plight of European Jewry. Maybe it would be more effective to approach a lower-level official, one who could respond more readily to an appeal to his sense of humanity.

The choice eventually fell on David Niles, an assistant to the President who happened to be Jewish. Niles was indeed stunned by the memorandum's contents and passed it on directly to General Dwight Eisenhower, the commander of Allied forces in Europe. Eisenhower was infuriated by the information and broadcast a tough message that threatened dire reprisals if the Germans carried through on their scheme. This had the desired effect, and the Jewish prisoners of war were spared.

FROM PAWNS TO KINGS

Though the hostilities ceased in 1945, the Vaad's work went on. If anything, it intensified. There were Jews throughout Europe, Asia and North Africa struggling to survive, seeking spiritual sustenance and searching for more accommodating shores.

The Vaad responded with an outpouring of aid and personal contact. Hundreds of thousands of dollars were rushed overseas; ten thousand dollars was sent monthly to supply kosher food to Sweden alone. From Teheran, the Vaad shipped sixty thousand parcels of food, clothing and religious articles; and more than one hundred thousand pounds of *matzos* were dispatched to Europe for *Pesach*. The Vaad also took the lead in reviving the educational system decimated by the Nazis. By 1948, it was supporting thirteen senior boys' *yeshivos*, sixteen Bais Yaakov schools and sixty-one Talmud Torahs and *yeshivos ketanos* just in Germany, and it had given out thirty thousand volumes of *Gemara*. Such Vaad representatives as Rabbi Shlomo Schonfeld, Rabbi Eliezer Silver, Mrs. Recha Sternbuch, Stephen Klein and Herbert Tenzer went overseas to bring both physical goods and liberal supplies of cheer and hope to the refugees. Others, like Mrs. Renee Reichmann, Dr. Yaakov Griffel, Rabbi Nathan Baruch and Rabbi Avigdor Vorhand, remained in Tangier, Turkey and Europe to carry out rehabilitation work on a daily basis.

One persistent problem involved bringing stranded refugees to safety in the United States. The immigration quotas were still in place, and even those granted visas were often unable to find the means of passage in the postwar turmoil.

It was in meeting these challenges that the ingenuity of leaders like Irving Bunim, inspired by Rabbi Aharon Kotler, often made the decisive difference.

A major concern of the Vaad was the welfare of the five hundred Torah scholars—half of them *rabbeim* and students from the Mirrer Yeshivah—who were still stranded in Shanghai, over five years after their arrival there. Attempts to transfer them to Sweden and Mexico had failed, and hopes centered on a relocation to America.

With returning servicemen receiving top priority, it took months for the Vaad to secure a ship that had space for such a large contingent. However, the old problem remained: the quota. The demand for visas was such that the chances of over five hundred European scholars gaining early entry to the United States seemed highly remote—unless the Vaad found champions who could help.

They did. The leading Vaad activists, including Rabbi Kotler, Rabbi Kalmanowitz, Irving Bunim, Stephen Klein and Herbert Tenzer, arranged a meeting with Under Secretary of State (and later full Secretary) Dean Acheson to discuss the issue. Bunim served as the delegation's spokesman.

"Mr. Acheson, our Sages taught that our leader Moses was the equal of six hundred thousand of his fellow Jews. Before you today sit two of our spiritual leaders who were able to escape the Nazis due to the kindness of the United States. Now over five hundred more are in Shanghai, wasting away in isolation. We need these leaders here; we need them to rebuild the world that the Nazis destroyed. We need them here to give new life to our people."

Bunim by now had tears in his eyes, but he didn't care what the staid officials thought. He went on. "We plead with you, sir. Help these scholars come to America, the land of the free. A battered but brave people will be eternally grateful."

Acheson let the words sink in. He was accustomed to hearing requests and pleas, but it wasn't often that he was appealed to on a spiritual basis. "Gentlemen," he said at last, "you don't have to worry. I will do all I can to help you and your rabbis overseas."

They were gratified but uncertain. Just what would this help consist of? How long would the Shanghai refugees still have to wait?

The answer was forthcoming. "I'll see to it that the quota restrictions for your group will be waived and that they won't have to worry about the standard physical entry exams. I'll get my trusted aide Cyrus Vance to take care of everything. So if everything works out as hoped, your rabbis might even be in the States before the Jewish holidays."

Acheson proved true to his word. The Shanghai contingent was in America in time for *Rosh Hashanah*, 1946.

The members of the Vaad delegation were overcome. "Your name will be engraved in gold letters in the annals of Jewish history," Bunim told Acheson as they departed.

The words proved to be more fateful than he knew.

A short while later, the Vaad tried to achieve similar results on behalf of several hundred rabbis from Russia and Germany who were stranded in Paris. The Vaad leaders hoped to expedite their entry into the United States and, in this regard, met with George Haering, chief of the State Department's Visa Division. Even before they could make their pitch, Haering announced that there was no way their request could be met. They left empty-handed.

Irving Bunim was dejected but not defeated. "I was just thinking of how helpful Acheson was, as compared to Haering, and I was wondering if we really showed him how grateful we were."

"Well, you did say his name should be written up in gold letters."

"Saying it is one thing, but . . . what if we followed through on that? Why don't we give him some tangible expression of gratitude, like a plaque or a scroll. It could even be in the form of a *megillah*, with his name actually written out in gold!"

So it was. The scroll was commissioned, with the tribute inscribed in ink on actual parchment, and Acheson's name spelled out in gold leaf. Vaad representatives returned to Acheson's office, but when his secretary agreed to give him the scroll, Bunim demurred. "It is a sacred article. If possible the rabbis here would like to bestow it on Mr. Acheson in person."

The Under Secretary finally appeared, and the presentation was made, with a blessing recited in Acheson's honor. He was deeply moved and pledged to speed up the processing of all visa applications involving rabbis. His intervention eventually helped cut the processing time by up to a year.

"What about the Jews stuck in Paris?" Bunim asked. "Can you sway Mr. Haering?"

"Why don't you present him with a scroll just like this? It might make all the difference in the world."

The delegation took up Acheson's suggestion—with great success. Haering was similarly impressed and, after consulting with Acheson, allowed the Paris group quick entry.

In postwar Switzerland, the problem was not one of immigration. Rather, it was a question of how to sustain the well-being of the refugees there. The indomitable Swiss rescue leader Mrs. Recha Sternbuch had been told that the Jewish refugees could remain in the country as long as the Vaad continued to feed and clothe them. This, however, was no easy task.

The Vaad turned to William O'Dwyer, then head of the War Refugee Board, to see if he could help in procuring and forwarding the necessary funds. O'Dwyer replied that his budget was stretched to the breaking point and that such long-ranged assistance would be impossible. Instead, he suggested that the Vaad approach Herbert Lehman, a Jewish former Governor (and future Senator) from New York, who was head of the United Nations Relief and Rehabilitation Administration at the time.

A Vaad delegation including Rabbi Kotler, Rabbi Kalmanowitz and Irving Bunim went to Lehman, who sadly turned them down. "You see," he explained, "Switzerland is not a member of the United Nations. Therefore, our agency is not in a position to send any supplies there."

The Jewish leaders were confounded. It seemed a bureaucratic nightmare, with no one willing to provide aid and the hapless Jewish refugees trapped in the maze. Reb Aharon, though, wouldn't let the others give up. "This is no time to stop. We must find a way to feed our desperate brothers, and if we work hard enough, Hashem will help us."

Shortly afterwards, Irving Bunim suddenly remembered that Herbert Lehman's legal advisor was Abe Feller, an old acquaintance of his. Maybe Feller could find a way out of the tangle.

Bunim went to see Feller, but the latter simply shrugged. "There is nothing to be done," he said.

But Bunim, heeding Reb Aharon's exhortations, wouldn't let it go at that. "Think of it this way," he said to Feller. "Let's say there was a fire right in the middle of the Brooklyn Bridge. The firemen are called, and the Brooklyn brigade says, 'But it's on the Manhattan side—let the firemen there put it out.' And the Manhattan brigade answers, 'No, it's the responsibility of the Brooklyn fire-fighters to do it.' They continue squabbling, and meanwhile, the fire keeps burning. Isn't that foolish?

"Now, here we have the same situation. The Refugee Board says they have the contacts but not the food, and the United Nations says they have the food but not the contacts. Meanwhile, no one is doing anything, and the Jewish refugees are starving! This is a dire emergency! There must be something you can do."

Feller considered for a while and then answered, "Let me work on it tonight."

The next day, he told Bunim that everything had been taken care of. The United Nations agency would send the food to the American Red Cross, which would pass it on to the International Red Cross, which would give it to the Swiss Red Cross, which would finally supply it to the needy Jews. It was a circuitous route, but it held.

One problem remained, though. The United Nations relief agency official wanted to know why only special, kosher food could be sent to the Jews, especially since this would prove more costly. Bunim replied that the Jews in need were very religious and that if they did not get kosher food they wouldn't eat.

The official's face lit up. "Oh, like in the book of Daniel!" he exclaimed.

Bunim sighed with relief. The man, a gentile, had recalled the story of how Daniel had refused non-kosher food while in captivity in Bavel. It made all the difference, and from that point on, the kosher food was delivered without any questions asked.

Not all refugee assistance involved such elaborate procedures. One day, some time after the war's end, Irving Bunim came to Reb Aharon's Boro Park apartment and was shocked by what he observed. The *rosh yeshivah*, who was normally submerged in his learning or preoccupied with *klal* work, was sitting in the living room, calmly playing a game of chess with a stranger.

This went on for some time, until the game finally concluded. Then the man smiled, shook Reb Aharon's hand and left. Reb Aharon turned to the greatly bewildered Bunim and offered an explanation.

"This man lost all he had in the holocaust, his family, his home, everything. When he came to America, he was so depressed he wouldn't talk. Someone asked me to speak to him. But what could I do? Talk in learning with him? He wasn't up to that. He did agree to play chess; that seems to soothe his nerves. So we play, and sometimes I throw in some encouragement. Let us hope it will help in the long run."

It did. The man eventually emerged from his personal fog and took an interest in life again. He found a job, remarried and built a new family. All from a game of chess.

From such seemingly minor moves, Reb Aharon knew, whole communities could be restored.

The Impossible Becomes Reality

Reb Aharon's zeal for saving lives was matched by his

perseverance in preserving life—the sacred lifestyle of his fathers and the very source of life itself: Torah.

There were those who mourned the intensive, all-consuming Torah study of pre-war Europe as an irretrievable casualty of the conflict. In Eretz Yisrael, with antiquity embodied in its very landscape, a few *yeshivos* of the old school might arise. However, in America, the very symbol of modernity, this was well nigh impossible. Granted, there might be Torah schools offering a mixture of religious and secular studies. But a *yeshivah* for post-high school students, and especially for married men, where the goal was learning Torah *lishmah*—for its own sacred purpose—was unheard of. American Jews were too pragmatic to allow their sons to delve into Torah day and night. Besides, the youths themselves, raised on materialistic values, would never go for it. Europe was the Old World, America was the New, and the twain would never meet.

Thus, when fourteen young Americans approached Reb Aharon in 1943 and requested that he become their *rebbe* in a new *yeshivah* modeled on the European *batei midrash* in which they had studied, Reb Aharon was perhaps a bit uncertain. Who would be willing to support such a unique American institution? But the students persisted, and Reb Aharon saw that some American Jewish youth were more spiritually inclined than their reputation allowed.

He characteristically accepted the challenge with full-fledged commitment. Rabbi Nissan Waxman, the Rabbi of Lakewood, New Jersey, helped secure a site for the *yeshivah*, but it remained an uphill battle. Potential donors were skeptical, and Reb Aharon and the laymen who assisted him had to assure them that America could indeed become a reservoir of pure Torah. There were numerous frustrations; doors were shut in their faces. Nevertheless, Reb Aharon never faltered in his crusade. He never told anything but the blunt truth. "We may produce *rabbanim* at our *yeshivah* and worthy teachers and *baalei batim*. But never doubt that the primary purpose of the institution is to create a love for undiluted Torah *lishmah*."

Like its European precursors, the *yeshivah* would be located outside a bustling metropolis, where its students would dorm and avoid the distractions of the big city. Lakewood was such a place, and starting with those first fourteen *talmidim*, Beth Medrash Govoha grew. It attracted more and more students, the brightest and the best, and acquired an impressive structure of its own. But it became not only a Torah center, but a spreading phenomenon. The *yeshivah* turned its home town into a recognized Torah community and established a precedent to be followed by others. The *kollel* was indeed feasible in America, and native-born American Jews could make Torah study the focal point of their lives.

For nineteen years and seven months, Reb Aharon stood at the helm of Beth Medrash Govoha, delivering *shiurim* with a fire derived from Heaven. The gaps dividing him from his *talmidim* were vast. They were so far apart in years, background and language. Yet, the gaps were bridged, through his personal concern for each and every student. To the young men, he personified the great sages of legend, in the guise of a father. They were loyal to him and, even more importantly, loyal to his ideals.

With Reb Aharon's passing in 1962, his son Reb Shneur inherited his mantle, for an equal tenure of nineteen years and seven months. Reb Shneur was a leader of a different manner—conciliatory rather than propulsive—but a leader nevertheless. Under Reb Shneur, the *yeshivah* expanded markedly, and today, under his son Reb Aryeh Malkiel, Beth Medrash Govoha has an enrollment of some two thousand five hundred students, in Lakewood and in the various branches it has established across America and throughout the world. Reb Aharon's legacy survives, and it thrives.

Yet, Reb Aharon's leadership was not limited to the

realm of the *bais midrash*. He was a natural *manhig*, a commander of men and promulgator of causes, and organizations clamored for his direction. Reb Aharon was a long time activist in Agudath Israel, dating back to his years in Europe; and upon the death of his good friend and colleague Rabbi Reuven Grozovsky, he was named head of the Agudah's Moetzes Gedolei Hatorah (Council of Torah Sages). He was also a chairman of Torah Umesorah and a leader of Agudath Harabbanim.

As such, he and his fellow *gedolim* grappled with many pressing issues confronting American and world Jewry. Sometimes, the decisions were controversial, but Reb Aharon held his ground. He was instrumental in rendering the *psak*, signed by himself and ten other leading *roshei yeshivah*, prohibiting Orthodox rabbis and rabbinical bodies from joining any organization groups with Reform and Conservative members. And he fought vigorously for federal aid for *yeshivos*, a stand denounced by many secular Jewish groups.

He also turned his sights to Eretz Yisrael, a land whose welfare concerned him deeply. He criticized the government's stands on religious issues, like drafting women, but he worked tirelessly to better the lot of Israel's Jews. As chairman of Chinuch Atzmai, and a strong supporter of Tashbar, he took an active part in their operations and raised money for them as vigorously as for his own *yeshivah*. All Torah institutions throughout the world were, in fact, beneficiaries of his interest and efforts.

Rabbi Chaim Soloveitchik had been right; this spiritual giant had indeed come to shoulder the burdens of his people. His unstinting activities on behalf of Torah and *klal* had been crucial in the replanting of the tenets and institutions of European Orthodoxy on American soil.

"We have one consolation," Rabbi Chaim Soloveitchik's son Reb Velvele, the Brisker Rav, noted after the full extent of the war's terrible toll on Torah Jewry became clear. "The

Almighty has left us Reb Aharon."

To our eternal benefit, the Almighty did spare this all-knowing, all-encompassing leader, and Reb Aharon in turn left us a legacy that keeps blossoming and expanding, and reminding us of a shining past that is, thanks to him, very much a part of our future.

An angel of Mercy

RABBI ELIEZER SILVER

A student of Rabbi Chaim Ozer Grodzinski in Vilna, Rabbi Eliezer Silver was one of the major rabbinical figures on the American Orthodox Jewish scene for over sixty years. Among other things, in 1939 he founded Agudath Israel of America, as well as Vaad Hatzalah. He was a true angel of mercy to the Holocaust victims, both during and after the War.

2 An Angel of Mercy

RABBI ELIEZER SILVER

TO SOME, HE SEEMED AN APPARITION, AN IMAGE OUT OF THE OLD, vanished order they had so dearly cherished. To others, he was a harbinger of the new, a promise of rediscovered hope and better days to come.

For everyone submerged in the rut of the Displaced Persons camp in Germany that summer of 1946, he was a startling but inspiring presence. Though he was short in stature, he looked ten feet tall in his sharp United States Army uniform, given to him for reasons of security. And though he was already sixty-five, and his beard was flecked with white, his sprightly walk and incisive speech made him seem youthful. The upbeat tempo of his words and his stride immediately gave a lift to the dispirited residents.

Reassurance and cheer were among the gifts that Rabbi Eliezer Silver brought along from America as he toured the European Displaced Persons Camps. Yet, he also came bearing tangible resources. There were food-stuffs that he liberally distributed, as well as much-needed clothing and personal items, letters from vaguely-known relatives in the United States, and many thousands of dollars. But the treasures that evoked the deepest-seated reactions were the religious articles, the reminders of a spiritual life the Nazis had tried to strip from their victims' psyches. And of these, the most precious was the very symbol of this sanctified life-a *Sefer Torah*. For the first time since the war had uprooted them, the members of the D.P. camps would have a *Sefer Torah* of their own. It would certify that the link between them and G-d had indeed survived.

To celebrate the return of the Torah to their fold, the Jews of the D.P. camp scheduled a special dedication ceremony. It emerged as an occasion for abundant joy and great somberness. A tide of pent-up emotions crashed through the hearts of those present. Smiles licked at flowing tears. Rabbi Silver, a gifted speaker and a great *talmid chacham* who could deliver orations with a flourish, did not need to produce a stemwinder this time. A few well-chosen words said it all.

For one D.P. inmate, a man in his mid-thirties, the emotions stirred by Rabbi Silver's visit were of a different order. He was bitter. Bitter at what had happened. Bitter at the Nazis, bitter at the Allies. And, most of all, bitter at his fellow Jews. He had openly announced to friends that he would not be attending the dedication. Deliberately. Out of anger and resentment.

Someone brought this to the attention of the valued guest. Rabbi Silver was not insulted. Instead, the night before the ceremony, he made it a point to stop by and chat with the estranged Jew.

"May I speak to you?"

The man was astonished to see the distinguished rabbi standing before him in the wretched barracks. Though he didn't know what a rabbi could possibly have to say to him, he reflexively nodded.

Rabbi Silver took a seat and introduced himself. He said

that he, too, had come from Eastern Europe and had then settled in America. But he felt a kinship with the European suvivors, and that was why he had come to see them and help them. But he had found that some Jews were angry and depressed. And apparently this man was among them.

"So tell me," Rabbi Silver said, as he put his hand on the other man's shoulder. "They say you are angry with G-d. Is that so?"

The man was not expecting that. Tensing to do battle with him, he looked for reproach in the rabbi's eyes. But he found only kindly concern.

"No, Rabbi," the man said, turning away. "I am not angry with G-d, but with His servants."

"You have suffered much."

"I have been through the labor camps and the extermination camps and the death marches. I have seen cruelty and savagery. But I expected it from the Nazi beasts. It is the treachery of my fellow Jews that I didn't expect—and that I will never forgive."

"Tell me about it. Please."

The man sighed with resentful memories. "It was at the Mauthausen death camp, at the end of the war. I had come from Buchenwald, just barely hanging on to life. What kept me going was the hope of a better world after the Nazis' fall, the pure world of my fathers. My fellow Jews would rebuild what had been lost.

"Then a train arrived at the camp, a train with Jews from Hungary. One was a pious-looking Jew, and he was assigned next to me. He had been through hell, but he still managed to persevere. Soon he told me what had kept him going. Concealed in his ragged clothing was a small *siddur*. Whenever he despaired, he took out the *siddur* and spoke directly to G-d. That gave him the will to survive.

"I must say, I greatly admired that man. It took courage for him to smuggle the *siddur* into the camp. He knew that if he was caught, he would be killed.

"But then something happened. Others also saw that he had the *siddur,* and they approached him. They hadn't seen a *siddur* in who knows how long, and they begged him to let them borrow it, for just a short time.

"'All right,' he told them. 'You can have it for a while—on one condition. Each time you borrow it, you have to give me a quarter of your soup ration.'

"Can you imagine, Rabbi? This? From a pious Jew? Using his pretense of faith to extort food from his fellow starving Jews! I could never forgive that. Never. And that is why I no longer want to have anything to do with the Jewish people. I'm sure you can understand that. Do you have any possible way to answer for the actions of that Jew?"

Rabbi Silver responded instead with a question of his own. "Can you tell me something? Did the other Jews take this man up on his offer?"

"Yes, in fact. Many of them did."

"Then, I hope you'll pardon me for saying so," Rabbi Silver went on, "but your attitude is dead wrong."

Was the rabbi adding insult to injury? "Excuse me, Rabbi."

"Let me explain," Rabbi Silver interrupted. "You say you were upset because this Jew took advantage of the situation. And you are certainly right. Some Jews might look religious, but they are far from religious at heart. Perhaps this man was so overcome with hunger that he didn't know what he was doing. Otherwise, I have no excuse for his behavior at all.

"But why are you focusing only on what *he* did? Why don't you consider the actions of the other Jews? Think of them. Here they were living on only a few pitiful scraps of food a day. And yet, they were willing to give up some of this precious food, just to be able to say the holy *tefillos* to Hashem. Can you think of a greater act of faith or a greater act of love?

"Nevertheless, you ignore all this, and concentrate on one misguided Jew. That is why I said you were so mistaken."

With that, Rabbi Silver patted the silent young man on the shoulder once more, and then left him alone with his thoughts.

The young man, whose name was Simon Wiesenthal, began to reconsider his sullen attitude. There were, indeed, two sides to issues, and the positive could sometimes counterbalance the evil. In the end, he decided to attend the Torah dedication and to view himself once more as a member of the Jewish people (though not as a truly observant one).

Later, as a world renowned Nazi hunter, Wiesenthal would help bring many of the Nazi murderers to justice. There were enormous obstacles and personal threats in seeking out these vile beasts. Many would strongly advise him to forsake his quest, and to let the undesirable ghosts of the past lie undisturbed.

Yet, Rabbi Silver's reminder was one of many factors that helped him persevere. There were, after all, so many good Jews who had perished at these butchers' hands, pure Jews whose dedication to G-d had surmounted all else. Their stories could not be forgotten, and their killers could not be absolved. Inaction born of depression or sulking would amount to nothing. One had to press on with the mission.

This devotion to action on behalf of his fellow Jews was Rabbi Eliezer Silver's credo, one he lived to the fullest. As a refugee new to the American scene, he confronted secularism and battled ignorance. As an Orthodox rabbi practicing in communities led by anti-religious Jewish clergy, he fought for recognition of Torah standards of law. And as a Jew living in safety while his European fellow Jews were facing doom, he moved heaven and earth to try rescuing them.

He was a fighter every minute of his life, a combattant for Torah with an acutely sharp mind and a ready response to crisis. Some who knew him called him "Quick Silver," and the name fit. But it was equally true that, at his core, he was pure gold.

ECHOES OF CHILDHOOD

The youngster cautiously took a sidelong peek out the window. He watched for only a moment, but the scene's impact lasted a lifetime.

There, right in front of his house, gentile thugs were raucously beating a Jew. They were reveling in their violence and flaunting their viciousness. "Down with the Yids," they sang in time to the beat of their poundings. And when they were finished with this victim, they searched deliriously for the next one. Meanwhile, the defenseless Jew lay groaning in the street.

He was only a child, but instinctively he felt the urge to help. Couldn't he do anything to stop these brutes from hurting his people?

But the time wasn't ripe for heroics. His father quickly pulled him away from the window, and hurried him to a sheltered room.

"It's not safe there," he informed young Eliezer. "We'll stay in here until the riot ends. And we'll pray to Hashem that it ends soon."

"But why?" The boy's searching eyes demanded some explanation.

"Do you remember the big fire we had here in Dusat a while ago?"

Eliezer nodded.

"Well, some of the gentiles heard a rumor that Mordechai set it," his father explained.

"Mordechai? The *shochet's* son? But why would he do that?"

"Exactly. He didn't. It's all a lie. But the gentiles believe it anyway. And that's why they started this pogrom."

"But I still don't understand," Eliezer persisted. "What do they have against us?"

"Nothing and everything," sighed his father. "Mainly, the fact that we are Jews. It's a matter of history. *Eisav soneih es Yaakov*. Eisav hates his brother Yaakov. You've learned that. It's something we have to live with as best we can. And we have to go on with our daily lives and our daily service of Hashem."

Daily life could be quite pleasant in the Lithuanian town of Dusat (located near Kovno), where Eliezer Silver's father served as *rav*. The Jews there formed a cohesive group, united in their observance and untouched by the assimilation running rampant in the large cities. Eliezer had been born in the nearby village of Abel on the 23rd of *Shevat* in 5641 (1881). His ancestry could be traced back to *David Hamelech* and included many distinguished *rabbanim*. Among them was Eliezer's paternal grandfather, who had served as *rav* of Dusat for half a century.

Rabbi Bunim Tsemach Silver, Eliezer's father, was a *talmid chacham* in his own right. Nevertheless, with a growing family to support, he chose to embark on a career in business. At the same time, he pursued his Torah studies at every available moment.

A scholar of this caliber was destined to lead his people. When his business began to falter, Rabbi Bunim turned to the rabbinate, and succeeded his father as *rav* of Dusat. It was here that Eliezer experienced his formative years—a time of quiet devotion to Hashem and intensive Torah study, punctured by the occasional eruptions of anti-Jewish agitation. Yet, even as he observed the flare-ups of the non-Jews, young Eliezer also learned how Jews could unite in countering the hatred. And his primary teacher in this matter, as in all others, was his father.

As *rav* of Dusat, Rabbi Bunim was kept apprised of

Jewish affairs not only in his own town, but also in neighboring villages. He was, therefore, one of the first to learn of young Chaya Menken's disappearance.

Chaya was an eight-year-old who lived with her family in a small hamlet near Dusat. Life could be drab for the youngsters there. There were no parks, and the few toys available would have to be shared by the many children in the family. Chaya sometimes sought recreation in playing outside the family dwelling. Her mother, tending to Chaya's younger siblings, gave her permission. "But be careful, and stay right near the house," she always cautioned. Chaya gave her solemn word. But her wanderlust often carried her far afield.

"Chaya!" her mother called. "Dinner! Come in right now!"

Normally, Chaya came running. This time, though, there was no response. Not even when her increasingly frantic mother called her name again and again. Her father joined in the search, and then their compassionate neighbors. Their investigation was exhaustive. But when night fell hours later, no trace of the girl had been found.

Then a visiting businessman offered a clue. Yes, come to think of it, he had seen a young girl fitting Chaya's description. Only she hadn't been alone. Someone had been leading her through the streets—someone clearly not Jewish. And they had been headed towards a neighboring town.

A kidnaping! Or more accurately, a religious abduction. This wouldn't be the first time that the non-Jews had grabbed a Jewish child in the hopes of baptizing him and weaning him away from Judaism. And experience had taught the Jews that, once stolen, a Jewish child was not easily regained.

Chaya's mother was overwhelmed with grief. Yet, the girl's aunt, refusing to abandon hope, concocted a plan of her own. Disguised as a non-Jewish woman, she took off for the neighboring town the visitor had mentioned. Boldly knocking on every door, and claiming to be searching for a lost object, she peered inside house after house, hoping for a glimpse of her niece.

Her persistence paid off. A rap on one door was answered by an old woman shrouded in black. The woman was visibly nervous; then, as the voice of Chaya's aunt rang out through the house, a child darted into view. *"Tante!* I'm here!"

Chaya's aunt wasted no time. The old woman tried to slam the door shut, but the combined action of Chaya and her aunt thwarted her efforts. Within seconds, Chaya was back in her aunt's loving arms, and the two fled from the house before the woman could summon help.

Chaya's reunion with her family seemed to resolve the issue. In fact, though, the struggle was just beginning. The non-Jews were outraged at the *chutzpah* of these Jews trying to snatch back their own child. After all, the girl had been baptized, and was no longer under Jewish jurisdiction.

A few days later, a mob began materializing in front of the Menken residence, led by a parade of priests. Their menace could not be ignored. Soon a chant rang out: "We want the girl!" As if a few sprinkles of water could make her theirs.

The clamor grew, until someone from inside the house felt compelled to come out and offer a response. That was the mistake the mob had been waiting for. With a shout, they surged into the house and grabbed Chaya, who was hiding inside, huddled with her mother. The crowd flung the older woman to the floor and made off with their prize—a girl crying hysterically for her mother. They would brook no dissent in the matter.

The family came to Rabbi Bunim, and he took decisive action. The size and power of the mob did not deter him. Seeking every legal means to get Chaya back once and for all, the *rav* began meeting with local officials and royal representatives. When palms were extended, he filled them with favors.

The bribes helped. After six months of intensive efforts, agreement was finally reached. Chaya was brought home, safe and sound. Not taking any chances, Rabbi Bunim made sure she was sent to live with relatives far from the reaches of the local crowds.

Only when Chaya was secure did Rabbi Bunim rest. Concerted action could save Jewish lives.

His young son watched, and learned.

THE DEVELOPING SCHOLAR

Eliezer's learning also encompassed the sea of *Talmud*, which his father helped him navigate. His remarkable memory and quick-witted insight, as well as his love of Torah, were key factors in his growing scholastic success.

By the time he was sixteen, his proficiency was such that his father thought him ready to join the prestigious *talmidim* studying in the city of Dvinsk. There he had the privilege of basking in the brilliance of Dvinsk's Torah luminaries, Rabbi Meir Simcha Hacohen (the Ohr Someiach) and Rabbi Yosef Rosen (known as the Rogatchover Gaon). After a year of intensive study, Eliezer moved on to Vilna and a new mentor— Rabbi Chaim Ozer Grodzenski. The vibrant *rebbe-talmid* bond that they forged was to have a major impact on the *hatzalah* work into which both men would be drawn.

In Reb Chaim Ozer, Eliezer found a giant of Torah scholarship and community leadership, one who led through the holy example of his own kindly modesty.

A master of all aspects of *Talmud*, Reb Chaim Ozer was the author of the noted *sefer*, *Ahiezer*, on Jewish law. The respect accorded him by Vilna's observant Jews was boundless, yet he refused an offer to become Vilna's Chief Rabbi, preferring instead the title "*Moreh Tzedek*," teacher of righteousness. He taught his eminent students, including Rabbi

Yechezkel Abramsky and Rabbi Shlomo Polachek, not only how to plumb to the core of Torah wisdom, but also how to apply that wisdom to serving the Jewish community.

Reb Chaim Ozer was always willing to answer *shailos* from the public, and played a leading role in such *klal-*oriented groups as Agudath Israel.

Eliezer Silver was electrified by the spirit of intensive study in Vilna and often learned for eighteen hours a day. His retentive mind absorbed all spheres of Torah learning; he mastered all four sections of the *Shulchan Aruch*, and was as well-versed in *Talmud Yerushalmi* as he was in *Talmud Bavli*. Reb Chaim Ozer wondered if someone that young could indeed have so complete a grasp of so many topics. When Eliezer responded to his questions with a display of Torah virtuosity, Reb Chaim Ozer was so overcome that he publicly embraced his student, calling him a leader of the future. After a brief stay in Brisk, where he studied under Rav Chaim Soloveitchik, Eliezer returned to Vilna, where he received *semichah* from Reb Chaim Ozer while in his early twenties.

NEW FAMILY, NEW DIRECTION

In 1906, Rabbi Silver married Bassia Aranowitz of Vilna, whose family included many Torah scholars. A year later, a son, David, was born, to be followed in 1910 by a daughter, Yetta, and, in 1912, the twins, Bessie and Nathan. But the joy coming from his burgeoning family was tempered by a troublesome development.

He was suddenly summoned to serve in the Russian army.

There were, to put it mildly, no *batei midrashim* within the Czar's army barracks. Those Jews who joined the Russian ranks were fortunate if they retained any Jewish identity after their service. Therefore, if enforced, this call-up would greatly complicate or even end Rabbi Silver's emergence as a Torah scholar.

He might have followed many of his peers and resorted to legal action (or a well-placed bribe) to fight the draft. Instead, in his boldly decisive way, Rabbi Silver chose another approach, one that was both challenging and potentially hazardous. He decided to move to America.

Some of his *chaveirim* had already made the voyage, with mixed results. If America was the land of opportunity, it was also a minefield of assimilation. Many a Jewish refugee from Europe had deposited his *Yiddishkeit* beside Miss Liberty's golden door, and succumbed to the pressure to "get ahead" by giving up his traditions.

Reb Chaim Ozer was therefore very reluctant to advise a move to this "*treife Medinah*." However, he knew that Rabbi Silver's strength of character and firm Jewish commitment would ensure his allegiance to Torah no matter where he was. Consequently, he gave his blessing to Rabbi Silver's relocation and presented him with a letter of reference. It read, in part, "His diligence was superb, and he developed into an expert in the entire *Talmud* and related studies. His high level of knowledge is equalled only by his deep love for Torah."

Upon arriving in New York, Rabbi Silver and his family were given generous accomodations by his wife's relatives. Through them, he also found employment as a salesman in the garment industry. Later, he sold insurance for a while. However, though this did pay the bills, it did not satisfy the soul. Rabbi Silver determined that he would not be held captive to economic needs. Instead, he would seek his true calling—the rabbinate.

He knew, though, that it would not be easy. The traditional rabbi seemed helpless to breach the fortress of Reform Judaism that had become entrenched in America. Even the refugees who clung to Orthodoxy were too contentious to accept strong rabbinic authority. The noted Rabbi Yaakov Yosef of Vilna, who had been brought over with much fanfare to serve as Chief Rabbi of New York, had died in 1902, a broken victim of American Jewish squabbles. Could Rabbi Silver adjust to the American ways without watering down his staunchly-held *yahadus*?

His first steps were tentative ones. He visited Jewish communities along the East Coast, familiarizing himself with the spirit of the inhabitants. The members of one community, Lithuanian refugees like himself, asked him to become *rav* of their *shul*. Though the offer was tempting, Rabbi Silver refused. He did not want to undermine the position of the *rav* already serving the area.

He was also offered a prestigious position with the newly-formed Jewish Theological Seminary. As yet unfamiliar with the Conservative movement, Rabbi Silver agreed to meet the Seminary's dean Solomon Schechter. Even before Schechter began explaining his school's philosophy, Rabbi Silver knew the Seminary was not for him. When Schechter greeted him, he was not wearing any head covering.

Then, in late 1907, with the help of Rabbi Bernard Levinthal, Rabbi Silver became the spiritual leader of the Orthodox congregations of Harrisburg, Pennsylvania—at a salary of six dollars a week.

Harrisburg was home to about two thousand Jews, many of them immigrants who had lost touch with their heritage. The fact that their new rabbi was a supreme Torah scholar didn't impress them.

It was quickly noted that the light in Rabbi Silver's study was on till all hours of the night. Clearly, he spent a great deal of his time poring over the *Talmud*, and some Jewish townsfolk wondered why this was necessary. "After all, when we hired the rabbi, we thought he was already smart," said one resident. "Then why does he always have to keep studying?"

As a result, the *Gemara shiur* that he instituted did not

find an abundance of attendees. Most were too ignorant or too uninterested.

One *shul* member had, in fact, been a gifted *talmid* of Rabbi Naftali Tzvi Yehuda Berlin (the Netziv) at the illustrious Volozhiner Yeshiva. However, the years had taken their toll, and the man's adherence to *mitzvos* had long since lapsed. Others in the city took their lead from his indifference to the law. Nevertheless, the *Talmud* still intrigued this man on an intellectual level, and his ties to the culture of the "Old World" lingered. When Rabbi Silver held a public *shiur* to celebrate his *shul* group's completion of a *mesechte*, the man attended. He was so impressed by the profundity of the discourse that he rethought his priorities. Soon, he was attending Rabbi Silver's *shiur* regularly and readopting the traditions of his youth. Others who noted this followed suit.

While bolstering the community's level of learning, Rabbi Silver was also strengthening its communal programs. He set up a *gemillas chessed* fund and a *hachnasas orchim* society, which assisted the impoverished refugees who kept arriving. Broadening his concerns to encompass the overall American Jewish scene, he joined his rabbinical colleagues in encouraging the observance of such neglected *mitzvos* as *Shabbos*, *kashrus* and *mikveh*. His growing Torah activism was recognized, and in 1912 he was elected to the executive committee of the Agudath Harabbanim, a national organization of Orthodox rabbis.

That same year, the Agudath Harabbanim chose him as one of a delegation formed to protest the treatment of Jews in Czarist Russia. One particular concern was the Russian government's policy of denying entry of Jews into the country without express consent from the Czar; violators were immediately arrested. The American government seemed to tacitly approve of this. It withheld passports from Jews seeking to travel to Russia until they had received permission from the Czar. Thus, Jews who wanted to visit their relatives there were effectively barred from doing so.

This was patently unfair. The rabbis sought to have this policy changed and to get American officials to pressure their Russian counterparts on their fellow Jews' behalf. Whom could they make their case to? Audaciously, they sought an appointment with President William Howard Taft himself and they got it. For the first time ever, a group of Orthodox rabbis would be meeting with the Chief Executive of the United States.

The encounter was set for June 12, 1912. En route to the White House, the *rabbanim* planned the thrust of the arguments they would present to the President. Then one other issue arose. It was a seemingly simple question: Should they keep their hats on during the meeting, in accordance with Jewish law? Or would President Taft interpret such behavior as being irreverent and therefore turn a cold shoulder to their cause?

The merits of each view were presented and weighed. Then Rabbi Silver asked to speak.

"I am firmly in favor of keeping our hats on. First of all, our respect for Hashem overrides our respect for any human leader, and I am sure He will intercede on our behalf. And second, this way, we will be able to recite the blessing over human rulers, '*Shenasan michvodo le'basar vadam.*' I am sure the President will understand our reasoning."

Rabbi Silver's argument was accepted. When the *rabbanim* were ushered before the hefty, genial Taft, they kept their hats in place. Then, to their dismay, they noticed that the President was glancing about in a preoccupied manner. He interrupted the meeting just as it was beginning and summoned an aide. Was he showing his displeasure?

The aide arrived, and Taft turned to him. "Could you do me a favor?" he said. "I'd like you to bring me my hat. I want to show my respect to G-d, too, just like these worthy gentlemen."

The rabbis relaxed, and the meeting proceeded successfully. It would not be Rabbi Silver's last encounter with major government officials.

A TASTE OF TROUBLES

By 1914, Rabbi Silver had come a long way towards establishing himself as a recognized force on the American Orthodox Jewish scene. Though he still retained a distinctive accent, he had become an American citizen, and he had begun to win national note as a *rav* who had developed a rapport with his American laity without forfeiting any of his religious principles. It was time, then, to fulfill a pledge made to his parents seven years earlier.

Before sailing off to America, he had promised to come back for a visit once he had settled down in his new homeland. Ever the dutiful son, he set off for Dusat after *Pesach*. There, he had a joyous reunion not only with his family, but also his *rebbeim*, the Ohr Someiach and the Rogatchover Gaon. Old memories were rekindled, and yet times had changed. The political atmosphere was highly charged. Rivalries among nations were festering, and when Archduke Franz Ferdinand of the Austro-Hungarian Empire was assassinated at Sarajevo, the fuse was lit. World War I broke out in August, 1914.

The conflict wreaked havoc among the populace of Europe, and especially among Europe's Jews. Centuries-old communities were devastated, religious life was disrupted, and *yeshivah* students were forced to study on the run. The toll on religious well-being was enormous.

World War I also posed a very immediate problem for Rabbi Silver. As a foreigner and a Jew, he suddenly came under suspicion. Claiming that the war had created a unique emergency, the Russian refused to recognize his passport. He had planned to be back in the United States by *Rosh Hashanah*.

Instead, he found himself stranded in Lithuania.

While trying to work out his legal difficulties, Rabbi Silver sought to reassure his wife and children back in the United States that he was well. However, phoning them proved impossible, and he feared that the government would censor any letters he might send. Therefore, he dispatched a heavily coded postcard, with veiled references to not being able to walk beyond the *techum* (a specific distance outside the city limits) on *Shabbos*. It was only when his fellow rabbis carefully studied the card that they deciphered the message.

In the meantime, Rabbi Silver was able to visit his beloved mentor in Vilna, Rav Chaim Ozer Grodzenski. The *gaon* was overjoyed to greet his *talmid* again, and their exchange of Torah thoughts buoyed the spirits of both. Yet, Rabbi Silver noticed the strain on Reb Chaim Ozer. Jews dislocated by the war poured into Vilna, desperate for help, and Reb Chaim Ozer was at the forefront of those tending to their needs. The great sage personally arranged for their lodging and food. He could not remain indifferent to the suffering around him.

Once again, Rabbi Silver became a student, keenly observing his *rebbe's* compassion.

As the visit drew to a close, Reb Chaim Ozer asked Rabbi Silver for a favor. "My dear Reb Eliezer, have faith. I know that Hashem will see to it that you return to America. You have a great opportunity there. Since the war has not touched America, you can accomplish much for your fellow Jews. See to it, won't you, that a fund is set up across the ocean to help out those in dire straits."

"I have certainly seen the suffering here with my own eyes," Rabbi Silver replied. "Yet, as the *rebbe* knows, there are already some groups helping the Jewish refugees."

"Perhaps, but they are secular groups. They do good work, but they will not understand the special needs of the Torah scholars. You are active in the Agudath Harabbanim.

They know what the Torah Jews will need. See what you can do, Reb Eliezer, and may Hashem bless your efforts."

Reb Chaim Ozer's assurances proved correct. Seven months after the war began, Rabbi Silver managed to slip across the border to neutral Norway. From there, he made his way back to Harrisburg.

The view of war had left an indelible impression on him. Immediately upon his return, he plunged into efforts to help the overseas refugees. And, to his delight, he learned that during his absence, the Agudath Harabbanim had come up with the very idea proposed by Reb Chaim Ozer. Thus was born the famous Ezras Torah organization to assist needy Torah scholars, and Rabbi Silver became its first vice chairman.

ON THE MOVE

In 1925, Rabbi Silver accepted an offer to serve as the *rav* of the United Orthodox Congregations of Springfield, Massachusetts. One of his first tasks there was to institute a strong central *kashrus* authority, a task he undertook with characteristic energy and speed. However, the success he achieved there quickly faced a serious challenge.

One of the Springfield butcher stores which was certified by Rabbi Silver was jointly owned by two brothers. One of them was a *shomer torah umitzvos*, while the other actively scorned religion. The observant brother saw to it that the meat sold in the shop was undeniably kosher, and under Rabbi Silver's *hashgachah*. But when the brothers quarreled, the religious one withdrew from the partnership, leaving his sibling as sole proprietor. After meeting with him and noting his contempt for *mitzvos*, Rabbi Silver promptly canceled his *kashrus* certification for the store. This resulted in a loss of business, and the man in turn sued Rabbi Silver. He claimed that the rabbi had illegally interfered with his business and caused him unwarranted monetary damage.

Ever the fighter, Rabbi Silver refused any out-of-court settlement. He forcefully argued that his decisive action had been both legally and morally correct. "After all, if anyone can just disregard a *kashrus* authority, what good is it? If we must, then let us go to court. Let us have our powers officially recognized." In the end, the courts agreed with him—and the victory was savored not only in Springfield, but in Orthodox Jewish communities throughout the country.

The case added to his prominence, as did his election in 1929 as president of the Agudath Harabbanim. Thus, Rabbi Silver was invited to visit Jewish communities throughout the country, to help arbitrate disputes and strengthen religious practices. On a number of occasions when religious issues resulted in lawsuits, he was asked to testify as an expert on Jewish law. In one such case, he dazzled even the non-Jewish judges and lawyers with his erudition. "Why, he just quoted one passage after another from the Jewish law books, entirely from memory!" one of them marveled. The world could now see just what a true *talmid chacham* was like.

Among the projects undertaken by Rabbi Silver was finding a *rav* for the Orthodox community of Cincinnati, Ohio.

The prospects for Orthodoxy thriving there seemed dim at best. True, there were several Orthodox *shuls* and an abundance of learned *baalei batim*. However, unity was elusive, and the incessant bickering had caused the previous *rav* to depart. Furthermore, Cincinnati had become a stronghold of Reform Judaism, and home to its seminary, the Hebrew Union College. Rabbi Silver arrived there in the spring of 1931 to see if there was any chance to remedy the situation.

After careful study, he recommended that a *vaad ha'ir* (Orthodox City Council) be created to unite the Orthodox community and promote a centralized *kashrus* authority. However, a strong rabbinical leader would be the key to the success of this venture.

The Orthodox lay leaders considered a number of possible candidates for this position, but each one drew objections. Finally, they came to a realization. The best qualified person had been right in their midst—Rabbi Silver himself! They had been awed by his decisiveness, zest and organizational abilities; the sermon he had delivered during his stay had been masterful. After the *Yamim Nora'im*, they wrote to him, imploring him to take the position. To bolster their cause, they asked the leaders of the Agudath Harabbanim to intercede on their behalf.

Rabbi Silver was reluctant to abandon his commitments to Springfield. Nevertheless, he realized that without strong leadership, Orthodoxy in Cincinnati might be doomed. Therefore, he decided to accept the offer. His installment took place in November, 1931, and a visiting *rav* commented, "Many have been led astray by the gold and silver edifices of the Reform movement. But they are only shiny buildings, containing nothing. However, you, dear congregants of Cincinnati, are fortunate, for you now have Rabbi Silver in your midst, and he is a true golden ornament for the Holy Torah." He would remain in their midst for the next thirty-seven years, until the end of his days.

Rabbi Silver brought to Cincinnati his singular brand of dynamic activism. He fought for a strong *kashrus* supervision and sought to have kosher accommodations in institutions like the local Jewish hospitals. He also led a drive for a new *mikveh*; the old one was located in a deserted neighborhood and was rarely used. Money was collected, and a site for the *mikveh* was purchased.

Then the drive faltered. Residents in the area—including several prominent Jews—declared their opposition to the *mikveh* being located in their neighborhood. Hiring a noted

Jewish lawyer, they filed suit to stop its construction, citing local zoning laws. The obstructionists claimed victory when the Zoning Board rendered a firm decision blocking the *mikveh*.

Those supporting the *mikveh* were resigned to defeat and prepared to seek a new location. They hadn't reckoned with Rabbi Silver's stubbornness. Instead of wavering, he turned to a leading non-Jewish politician and lawyer, Robert Taft, the son of the President that Silver and the other rabbis had visited twenty years earlier. The younger Taft proved just as accommodating as his father had been. He saw this as an issue of freedom of religion and agreed to represent the *mikveh* proponents in court. At Taft's request, Rabbi Silver prepared a detailed report on the importance of the *mikveh* in Jewish life to buttress the case.

As soon as this turn of events became known, opponents of the *mikveh* conceded defeat. They withdrew their objections, and the *mikveh* project went ahead as planned.

Soon after, Rabbi Silver received a bill of four thousand dollars for Taft's services. Enclosed with it was a receipt, stating, "Paid in full."

Rabbi Silver was most grateful for Taft's generous assistance. He would turn to him again when Taft was a powerful Senator, and Rabbi Silver needed help securing not *mikvaos* but Jewish lives.

OMINOUS NEWS

While enjoying these professional successes, Rabbi Silver suffered a great personal loss when Bassia, his wife of twenty-eight years, passed away in 1935. Both he and the Jewish community mourned her deeply, and the Bassia Silver Free Loan Fund was established in her memory. Four years later, the gloom that had darkened his life lifted when Rabbi

Silver was married to Pearl Berkson, whose devotion and support were indispensible to him for the next three decades, until his death.

In addition to his role in the Agudath Harabbanim, Rabbi Silver played a prominent part in the establishment of Agudath Israel in America. This European-based organization, which worked for the welfare of the Orthodox community under the guidelines of the *gedolei hador*, had not really taken root in the United States, although its youth branches, Pirchei and Zeirei, had begun functioning under the leadership of Reb Elimelech ("Mike") Tress. However, in 1939, Rabbi Silver was instrumental in formally establishing an American branch of the Agudah, and at its first convention in Far Rockaway, New York, he was elected president. Thus, at a time when plane travel was slower and hardly the norm, Rabbi Silver became a constant flyer. He thought nothing of the taxing schedule of flying from Cincinnati to New York and then back again in order to conduct business on behalf of *Klal Yisrael*.

Earlier, in 1937, he had heeded the urging of his *rebbe* Rabbi Chaim Ozer Grodzenski and crossed the Atlantic by boat to attend the Agudah's *Knessiah Gedolah* in Marienbad, Austria, as leader of the American delegation. His first stop on the journey was in Vilna, where he once again had the coveted privilege of spending an unforgettable *Shabbos* in Reb Chaim Ozer's presence. At the *Knessiah*, he had the further pleasure of meeting such Torah luminaries as the Gerer Rebbe, Rabbi Elchanan Wasserman of Baranovitch and Rabbi Menachem Zemba of Warsaw. Asked to address the assemblage, he importuned the *rabbanim* of Europe to forge closer ties with the American Jewish community and impart their spirit of Torah greatness to their Jewish brothers overseas.

No one present could know that this would be the last such gathering of European Torah giants ever.

Within a few years, Reb Chaim Ozer would be gone; the Gerer Rebbe and others would be fleeing for their lives; and both Rabbi Elchanan Wasserman and Rabbi Menachem Zemba would be counted among the many *gedolim* who gave their lives *al kiddush Hashem* during the Nazi massacres.

The powerful emotional bond that Rabbi Silver had established with the European *rabbanim* was one factor that spurred him to fight so fiercely for their rescue.

The German invasion of Poland in September 1939 brought war and untold misery for Polish Jewry. Through his enduring correspondence with Reb Chaim Ozer, Rabbi Silver gained a vivid picture of the rapidly deteriorating situation.

When Russia took over Eastern Poland that fall, as stipulated by the Russian-German non-aggression pact, it also forced Poland to return the city of Vilna to Lithuanian auspices. (See Volume I, Chapter 2, for details.) This unexpected development allowed some twenty thousand Jewish refugees, including nearly three thousand *bnei yeshivah*, to slip across the Polish-Lithuanian border to the relative safety of Vilna. There, they continued their Torah studies under the kindly supervision of the spiritual father of all *yeshivos*, Reb Chaim Ozer.

Caring for this sudden influx of refugees was no simple task. This being wartime, food was scarce. Nevertheless, the Vilna Jewish community managed to provide for the newcomers as best they could. Their efforts were overseen by Reb Chaim Ozer, even though he was often bedridden with the stomach cancer that would eventually claim his life. Reb Chaim Ozer saw to it that the *bnei yeshivah's* basic needs were met without their having to disrupt their learning. Yet, the resources of the Vilna Jewish community were far from boundless. Additional aid was needed, at once.

Reb Chaim Ozer knew whom to approach for help. Earlier, he had told Rabbi Silver, "It is clear that Hashem inspired you to emigrate to the United States for a purpose. The Jews of America are the ones who can provide for their poor brothers over here. It is your role to make them see that."

Now was the time for that role to be played out. The close-knit ties with European Jewry, the empathy he shared with bereft war refugees, the strong ties he had developed with community and political leaders, and the very tenacity of his character—all these made Rabbi Silver the perfect man of action for this time of crisis.

On *Rosh Hashanah*, 1939, Rabbi Silver received a telegram from Reb Chaim Ozer, a sure sign that an emergency was unfolding.

"Students are streaming into Vilna from all over Poland. Their learning continues, but they must be fed. Help is needed as soon as possible! Have all American Jews heed our cry, and may you all be blessed!"

Rabbi Silver responded immediately. He called an urgent meeting of his fellow *rabbanim* at the New York office of Agudath Harabbanim, and the attendees issued a fervent plea for funds:

"The rescue of the *yeshivos*," it read in part, "will demand tremendous financial help from us. It is *essential* that we offer our speedy aid to the students and to the Torah teachers, those heroes who have shown so much devotion and self-sacrifice. We must give all we can, right now!"

That, however, was only the first shot in the struggle to help the *yeshivos* survive. Additional ways to accomplish this goal were explored, and an emergency convention of hundreds of *rabbanim* was held in November. They all agreed that extraordinary measures had to be taken, but the question was one of procedure. Some *rabbanim* felt that aid could be funneled through existing organizations, like Ezras Torah or the secular Joint Distribution Committee. Rabbi Silver disagreed.

"What is called for is a new organization, one created specifically to help the *yeshivos* during this crisis. We cannot expect the secular Jews to understand the special needs of the Torah scholars. If we want to see them get the type of aid they deserve, then we, the religious Jews of America, have to offer it ourselves."

This view was adopted, and the Vaad Hatzalah was born.

It was Rabbi Silver who saw to it that the Vaad remained an independent body, officially unalligned with any religious group. Though he himself was the president of Agudath Israel, he preferred not to have Vaad Hatzalah fall under the Agudah's banner. That way, the Vaad's fundraising drives could appeal to Jews belonging to all groups—especially important since, at that time, most Orthodox *shuls* were firmly in the Mizrachi camp.

For the next seven years, the Vaad was to perform extraordinary service on behalf of the imperiled Jews of Europe, both during and after the war. Though Orthodox Jewry was still a minor, disorganized force in the United States, this Orthodox organization was to play the pivotal role in American *hatzalah* efforts during the Holocaust. Originally formulated to aid the endangered *bnei Torah*, Vaad Hatzalah eventually came to work energetically for the rescue of all of Hitler's designated victims.

VAAD HATZALAH AT WORK

The army of religious activists may have been small, and their resources—both financial and political—severely limited. However, led by such generals as Rabbi Silver, Rabbi Avraham Kalmanowitz of the Mirrer Yeshiva (who came to the United States in 1940) and Rabbi Aharon Kotler (who arrived in 1941), as well as lay leaders like Irving Bunim and Elimelech Tress, they quickly advanced on several fronts.

Intensified fund raising was a natural priority. However, the leaders of the Vaad wanted to ascertain just how to put the money to best use. To that end, they designated a representative to visit Vilna and consult with Reb Chaim Ozer, in order to coordinate the relief effort with him.

The person they chose for the task was Dr. Samuel Schmidt, an acquaintance of Rabbi Silver who was the editor of a Jewish weekly in Cincinnati. Schmidt was not originally a *shomer mitzvos*, but under Rabbi Silver's tutelage, his religious observance had increased. Despite the risks involved in the trip, Schmidt agreed to undertake it, because he had been asked by Rabbi Silver. "I would do anything he says," Schmidt remarked, "because his words are holy to me."

Schmidt arrived in Vilna at the end of February, 1940, and his first act was to meet with Reb Chaim Ozer and delineate his mission. The *gadol* listened intently, and after he had finished, he said, "It is a great privilege to have you in our midst. Do you mind if I ask a favor of you?"

"Certainly, Rabbi. That's why I am here. What would you like?"

"Would you permit me to call you 'Reb Shmuel'?"

Schmidt was flabbergasted. Here was this remarkable sage, revered by religious Jews everywhere, asking for permission to address him—a not-fully committed Jew—as a colleague! "But rabbi, I am certainly not worthy of such a title."

"Ah, but I think you are," Reb Chaim Ozer replied. "After all, you voluntarily left the comfort of your home in America and endangered yourself, just to see to our welfare. For someone like that, no title can do you justice."

Schmidt was so overwhelmed that he decided then and there to become a fully practicing Jew. As "Reb Shmuel," he could do no less.

For the next three months, Schmidt visited the Torah scholars still studying intensively in the Vilna area. There were some three thousand of them, and each *yeshivah*—Mir, Kletzk, Radin, Baranovich, Kamenitz and Bialystok—retained its individual approach to learning as Reb Chaim Ozer had stipulated. Wherever he went, Schmidt noted their dire needs, and distributed the funds that the Vaad had provided him. He returned to the United States in June, 1940, carrying with him Reb Chaim Ozer's stark request: "*Save the living Torah of Europe!*"

Soon the plea took on added urgency. In July, 1940, Russia ordered a takeover of Lithuania, and the fate of Vilna's Jews was sealed. *Shechitah* was outlawed; the city's Vaad Hayeshivos was closed down.

Reb Chaim Ozer's strength was ebbing. Nevertheless, he took pen in hand and began a letter to Rabbi Silver, outlining the latest needs.

His companions noticed the *gadol* wincing in pain. "Perhaps the Rav would prefer to dictate the letter instead," one suggested.

"No," said Reb Chaim Ozer. "Maybe if Rabbi Silver sees these words in my own shaky writing, he will see how desperate we are."

It was the last letter Reb Chaim Ozer would compose. By the time Rabbi Silver received it, word had spread that the spiritual leader of Vilna's Jews–and of all *Klal Yisrael*–had passed away, on the 5th of *Av*, 1940.

With Reb Chaim Ozer's death, the situation deteriorated further. The head of the Brisk Yeshivah wired frantically, "Our students hunt for bread, and we do not have the means to sustain them. Every hour that our aid from you is delayed intensifies the danger to life; it also increases the time spent away from Torah study. All our local sources of income have vanished."

The "living Torah of Europe" faced total obliteration. Could anything be done?

Highest priority was given to spiriting Vilna's scholars out of Europe. Tragically, this proved inordinately difficult. The United States government, still officially neutral, had restrictive immigration quotas and guarded them strictly. The British, intent on appeasing Arabs, cut off entry into Palestine. Circumventing these laws was nearly impossible, but the

Vaad did everything it could to rescue the *bnei Torah*.

One approach was to try to bring them over as clergy-men already assured of jobs in the United States. Thus, Rabbi Silver asked *shuls* in Cincinnati to send employment contracts to *rabbanim* in Europe. A number were permitted entry based on this. Rabbi Zalman Sorotzkin, the Lutzker Rav, was one of those offered help in this way, though he eventually managed to secure passage to Eretz Yisrael.

Another who did so was the Gerer Rebbe, Rabbi Avraham Mordechai Alter, mentor of thousands of *chassidim*. When it was first apparent that the *rebbe*, a primary target of the Nazis, was in danger, Rabbi Silver took action. He contacted his old acquaintance Robert Taft, now a powerful U.S. Senator from Ohio. Taft, in turn, got in touch with Secretary of State Cordell Hull, who tried unsuccessfully to locate the *rebbe*. It was later determined that he had fled to Warsaw; and Rabbi Silver joined others in applying pressure for the *rebbe's* successful entry into the Holy Land.

Others were able to get entry visas to the United States on their own, but were stymied at finding money to pay for their passage. Here again, Rabbi Silver played a vital role.

One day, Rabbi Silver's overburdened schedule was interrupted by an unannounced visitor, a man who identified himself as a rabbi from Brooklyn, who held out a picture before him. "You don't know me, Rabbi Silver, and you don't know the young man in this photo. But I was told you might be of some help."

Rabbi Silver gazed at the photo and saw before him a young man staring intently into an open *sefer*.

He put aside his other work and asked the man to sit down. "Please, how can I help you?" Everything else could wait.

"He's a friend of mine from Poland, who's been learning in the Mirrer Yeshivah," the rabbi explained. "I got out, but he's still trapped in Europe. He has the papers to come here, but no way to pay for it. Can anything be done?"

"I certainly hope so." Rabbi Silver picked up the phone, contacted his travel agent and explained the situation. The agent said that he would sell the *bachur* a ticket to America at half price. "Fine. Then charge the rest to my account."

The young man, Elya Chazan, arrived in the United States some time later, and he became a *rosh yeshivah* at Mesivta Torah Vodaath. The Brooklyn rabbi sought to express his appreciation to Rabbi Silver for his assistance.

"No," said Rabbi Silver, "it is I who must thank you for allowing me to take part in this great deed of rescuing a Torah scholar."

Others survived, too, due to a confluence of developments that were recognized afterwards as being nothing short of miraculous. Suddenly, the normally restrictive Russians allowed many Vilna refugees to depart. By chance, from an honorary Dutch consul named Jan Zwartnik, they secured artificial but crucial end visas to Curacao which proved fully effective. A sympathetic Japanese consul in Kovno named Senpo Sugihara prepared transit visas for them to Japan. All that was needed were the funds for the trip out of Russia, and through superhuman efforts by Rabbi Kalmanowitz, Rabbi Silver, Irving Bunim and others, these were raised in time. By the end of 1940, over a thousand Jewish refugees, including close to six hundred *bnei yeshivah* (half of them from the Mirrer Yeshivah) had made it safely to Kobe, Japan. (For a lengthier description of this incredible escape, see Volume I, Chapter 2.)

In the case of individual *rabbanim*, the Vaad Hatzalah was able to secure their entry to America, despite the restrictive quotas. A representation of Vaad leaders, including Rabbi Silver and Rabbi Kalmanowitz, visited Washington in a quest for immediate visas for their desperate European colleagues. (The Roosevelt administration had agreed to allow in a limited number of distinguished refugees with Emergency Visitors

Visas.) Assistant Secretary of State Breckinridge Long, who was not known for his partiality to the cause of Jewish immigration, agreed to meet with them. He asked that they prepare two lists: one of a hundred *rabbanim*, and one of only twenty, who should receive priority treatment. The arguments of the delegation made such an impression on him that he accepted the longer list and promised to do what he could. Five hundred visas were subsequently issued, but by then it was too late for all but forty of them to be used. Nevertheless, a number of prominent Torah leaders did make it to America during the war, including Rabbi Reuven Grozovsky, Rabbi Avraham Yoffen, Rabbi Eliyahu Meir Bloch, Rabbi Moshe Shatzkes, Dr. Isaac Lewin and Rabbi Aharon Kotler.

Reb Aharon, the *rosh yeshivah* of the Kletzk Yeshivah and the future founder of Lakewood's Beis Medrash Govoha, arrived in the United States from Kobe on April 10, 1941. Soon after, he traveled to Cincinnati, where he stayed with Rabbi Silver.

Rabbi Silver accompanied Rabbi Aharon Kotler to New York and introduced the *rosh yeshivah* to a large crowd of Orthodox well-wishers (mainly Pirchei and Zeirei Agudath Israel youth) at Pennsylvania Station: "My dear friend, the great *gaon* Rav Aharon Kotler is the greatest teacher of Torah in our generation. I am certain that he will raise the level of Torah in America and that we will now be able to educate great Torah scholars here. May his coming be for peace and success."

It was, indeed. Reb Aharon immediately joined Rabbi Silver and Rabbi Kalmanowitz at the helm of the Vaad, and with his energetic imput, the work of Vaad Hatzalah took on a new impetus and urgency in an atmosphere of greater Jewish unity.

THE WORK INTENSIFIES

In August, 1941, the Japanese government began relocating the Jewish refugees from Kobe to the international city of Shanghai, which it controlled. There was hope that this would prove a springboard for transferring them *en masse* to America, Canada or Eretz Yisrael. However, in December, 1941, the Japanese bombed Pearl Harbor, and with war underway, all ties between Japan and the United States were cut.

The hundreds of *bnei yeshivah* in Shanghai were among the four hundred thousand Jewish refugees there who now found themselves cast adrift. All aid from America was officially prohibited. How could they live, much less learn?

Perhaps there were ways to skirt the legal ban. Here, though, the Vaad faced extensive opposition. By far the largest and most efficient Jewish relief organization was the American Joint Distribution Committee (the JDC), which had provided substantial aid to Jewish refugees throughout the world. Now that the United States had entered the war, the JDC cut back. The law was clear: there was no dealing with the enemy–even if Jews remained behind enemy lines. There was no choice. Support for the Shanghai Jews would, sadly, have to stop.

Could the Vaad stand up to the JDC? Could a mosquito, however persistent, take on an elephant?

The leaders of the Vaad had tried it once before. With millions of helpless Jews under German domination, Agudath Israel had begun sending food packages to the trapped and starving Jews. However, this ran afoul of the policy of some well-meaning secular Jewish groups, which had formed in 1936 a Joint Boycott Council. The goal was to isolate Nazi Germany even before the war by promoting a ban on all exchanges between it and the United States. The Council applied this to the food packages as well, and when the

Agudah continued to ship the parcels, it took action. On July 15, 1941, the Council began picketing Agudath Israel offices. Jews fighting Jews out to help other Jews! The Agudah stubbornly refused to submit and continued shipping these vital packages. However, when British officials threatened to arrest Jewish refugees in England if the shipments continued, the Agudah had no choice but to capitulate. It followed the dictates of Jewish law stating that one life was just as precious as another; therefore, the Agudah had no right to jeopardize the lives of British Jews through their actions.

This time, though, there was no backing down. Aid had to be funneled to the Shanghai Jews, and a route was found. It depended on the transfer of funds to neutral Switzerland, where the ever-helpful Sternbuchs were waiting to ship it to Shanghai via their HIJEFS organization. Rabbi Avraham Kalmanowitz took the initiative in gaining official American sanction for this linkup (see Volume I, Chapters 2 and 5).

The Jews in Shanghai were not the only ones at the receiving end of the Vaad's beneficence. Those in Vilna who had not been able to escape to Kobe in 1940 were among the many thousands of Jews rounded up by Russian troops and shipped to Siberia in mid-1941. This seeming catastrophe had retrospectively developed into a piece of good fortune: Immediately after the expulsion, the Nazis invaded Russia and slaughtered all Jews in their path. Had the Siberian Jews not been taken away, they, too, would have perished.

However, coping with the duress of a Siberian winter was no delight. Funds were needed for these Jews, too. And what of those Jews still consigned to cramped and fetid conditions in ghettos throughout Europe?

The Vaad began to expand from a minor group aiding selected *rabbanim*, to a respected organization that sought the rescue of all European Jews. Its rabbinic leaders and their lay assistants outdid themselves crisscrossing the country and appealing for funds. Rabbi Silver's enormous drive and stamina served him well in that regard. (Years later, a Lakewood Yeshivah student related how he had accompanied Rabbi Silver on a fundraising mission for the Yeshivah. Though Rabbi Silver was three times his age, the man could hardly keep up as the two visited one potential benefactor after another. Back in their hotel room, Rabbi Silver asked his companion to learn with him until 2 a.m.; the next morning, the young man awoke to find Rabbi Silver already refreshed and immersed again in the *Talmud*. They then journeyed to New York, from where Rabbi Silver went on to his next appointment, while the young man headed straight to his bed for a few days of recuperation.)

The efforts bore fruit. In its first campaign, in 1941, Vaad Hatzalah raised some eighty thousand dollars. By 1944, though, it had expanded that sum to over *a million dollars* (worth a hundred times that amount today), making it second to only the well-established JDC among all Jewish relief groups. Considering that the basic constituency of the Vaad were Orthodox Jews, who were far from affluent in the 1940s, that was a remarkable achievement.

Nevertheless, the Vaad, or any Jewish group, could do only so much on its own. Forcing the Nazis to cease their murderous targeting of Jews would require pressure on a governmental level.

With that in mind, Rabbi Silver kept firing off letters and telegrams to national leaders throughout the war to Roosevelt, Stalin and even the Pope. Nothing seemed to help.

By 1943, though, the tide of the war had turned. With America unleashing its mighty firepower, and Russia turning the Germans back at Stalingrad, the Nazis were finally tasting defeat. Could the Allies use this advantage to win concessions from Germany on behalf of the beleaguered Jews? Could they commit themselves to saving what was left of European Jewry?

With the convening of the Bermuda Conference on April

19, 1943, the *hatzalah* workers took heart. Finally, the Americans and British were meeting specifically to deal with the plight of the war refugees. Surely the results would benefit those singled out for destruction by the common enemy.

Not at all.

The first sign that the conference would be a farce came with the announcement that no private organizations would be allowed to attend. The Americans and the British would decide the refugees' fate on their own. Then, since it was up to them, these governments took the course that served them best—no action at all. America would take in no additional Jews, and England would keep the doors to Palestine shut. There wasn't even any acknowledgment that the Jews were the Nazis' primary victims. The only result was a hazy suggestion that perhaps some refugees could eventually be housed in North Africa.

The Jewish leaders were dumfounded. "Now we understand our rabbis' teachings not to place our faith in human leaders," said one.

Rabbi Silver, though, was not content to let matters rest there. If the United States government was unwilling to rise to its moral responsibilities, he would try to stun it into action.

Through Irving Bunim, Rabbi Silver had met Peter Bergson. Bergson, the nephew of Chief Rabbi Avraham Kook of Eretz Yisrael, was not an observant Jew, but he strongly believed in the unity of the Jewish people. As a Revisionist Zionist and a follower of Vladimir Jabotinsky, he opposed the views of the Socialist Zionists who promoted immigration to Eretz Yisrael to only young, Zionist-oriented secular Jews. The Revisionists pushed for the admittance of *all* Jews to the Holy Land. In this, Rabbi Silver found common cause with the group. He also admired their willingness to fight the secular Jewish Establishment's policy of remaining silent and thereby not gaining unwanted attention. Bergson and his followers openly chided the Allies for their indifference to the Jews' plight, and publicized their views through newspaper ads and public presentations.

Working with the Bergson group, Rabbi Silver and the members of the Vaad took a daring step. They organized a March on Washington to demonstrate for greater action by the American govenment on behalf of Jews remaining under Nazi domination. Some advised the Vaad to think twice about the march. It would attract too much attention, and would put the Jews too visibly in the forefront. But that was exactly what Rabbi Silver wanted. Quietly waiting for the Allies to act on their own had led to nothing.

Therefore, on October 6, 1943, the day before *Erev Yom Kippur*, the nation's capital became the site of an unprecedented scene. Some four hundred rabbis marched from Union Station to the Capitol Building, with Rabbi Eliezer Silver in the forefront.

The rabbis had requested a meeting with President Franklin D. Roosevelt to present their case. However, Roosevelt was at heart a politician rather than a humanitarian. Loathe to champion Jewish issues, he heeded the advice of one of his close Jewish advisors, Judge Samuel Rosenman, not to greet the marchers: "Believe me, Mr. President, they're only a group of old-fashioned rabbis. They don't represent the views of the real Jews of this country."

Instead, Roosevelt sent Vice President Henry Wallace, who listened as Rabbi Silver read, in Hebrew, a Rescue Memorandum which another rabbi presented in an English version.

"In this time of emergency," it said in part, "it is a sacred duty for this government to take urgent measures for saving the Jewish people by: a) finding a way to immediately stop the mass killings by the Nazi murderers; b) warning the German people that the murder of the Jews will not be forgotten, while rescue activities will be given due recognition; c) sending food and medical help to Jews in the ghettos, to be distributed by a neutral commission or the International Red Cross; d) influencing neutral countries to give Jewish refugees a safe haven; e) easing the immigration quotas and allowing a greater number of refugees to enter the U.S.; f) immediately opening the gates of the Land of Israel, the Holy Land of our fathers, to Jewish immigration; and, most importantly, g) establishing a special agency for rescuing the remnants of the Jewish people in Europe.

"We pray to G-d Almighty that the President of the United States will recognize this historic moment of great responsibility in which he was chosen by the Creator to save many people together with the remnants of the Eternal People of the Book.

"For this, may G-d Almighty help us to reach a quick victory on all fronts in the struggle against our enemies and in the effort to achieve peace."

Speaker of the House Sam Rayburn and other influential lawmakers also met with the delegation, and the march left a forceful impression on them. The resulting political and public pressure was one of the factors that led at last to the creation of the War Refugee Board on January 22, 1944. This was the American government's sole agency devoted to saving and assisting refugees, and its formation came woefully late. Millions were already dead; only thousands remained. Nevertheless, the War Refugee Board did achieve some noteworthy successes and provided a means through which the Vaad Hatzalah could transfer funds from America to the Sternbuchs in Switzerland for rescue purposes.

In another late and limited act of sympathy, the American government allowed close to a thousand refugees to enter the United States on a temporary, emergency basis. Arriving from Italy, they were admitted to Fort Ontario, an abandoned army base near Oswego, New York. The group included three hundred Orthodox Jews led by Rabbi Mosco Czechoval, and the Vaad saw to it that they were supplied with such religious necessities as *talleisim*, *tefillin*, a Talmud Torah for the children and kosher food. When word spread among the refugees that the kosher food was superior to the standard fare, even the non-religious Jews requested it. The Vaad readily and happily provided it.

The Orthodox refugees then approached the Vaad for an additional favor. They wanted a *mikveh* built on the premises. A delegation consisting of Rabbi Silver, Irving Bunim, Isaac Lewin and Yitzchak Furstenberg met with Joe Smart, the director of Fort Ontario, to gain permission for the request. There was one hurdle to overcome first—explaining to Smart just what a *mikveh* was.

"It is a bath where Jewish people immerse themselves for ritual purposes," Rabbi Silver noted.

"Ah, I see," said Smart. "You want a swimming pool."

"No, not exactly," Rabbi Silver went on. "This isn't meant for pleasure. You see, a *mikveh* has to be built according to clear-cut rabbinic specifications. For instance, it must have at least forty *seah* measures of water."

"And a *seah* is?"

"It's a liquid measurement. And the *mikveh* must be filled with natural water."

"But isn't all water natural?"

"No, this means *still* water. It must come from the sky or the river, not a pipe or a faucet. And the *mikveh* is measured in *amos*, and an *amah* is—"

"Wait!"

Smart threw up his hands in frustrated exasperation. He turned to one of the camp engineers. "Do whatever the rabbi says," he ordered. "I just hope you understand it. I certainly don't."

Rabbi Silver didn't give up, and somehow the *mikveh* was built within two weeks.

The experience of providing for the Oswego Jews was providential. As the war reached its climax, it became clear that the Vaad's work would have to be redirected. With the

Nazis about to be driven from power, attention focused on how to service the war's survivors.

COURIER OF COURAGE

May 8, 1945 saw an end to the war in Europe, but not to the suffering there.

Enmeshed in the rubble of the continent were some four hundred thousand ragged Jews, some emerging from the traumas of hiding, others staggering out of the concentration camps more dead than alive, and yet others returning from exile in Siberia and central Asia. Their families had been splintered, their loved ones butchered, their property confiscated, their institutions obliterated. Many were languishing in Displaced Persons Camps in Germany, bereft of ties to their heritage. Others were dazedly returning to their old communities, only to find themselves still labeled unwanted intruders. The most tragic of all were the children who had been sheltered by Christian families who now showed no inclination of returning them to their rightful families.

Shortly before Germany's surrender, Rabbi Silver said the following to an assemblage of the Agudath Harabbanim:

"In our cycle of weekly Torah readings, we are up to *Acharei Mos* ("After the Death"). The significance of this is obvious.

"We have learned the dreadful news that more than five million of our brothers and sisters have been slaughtered. [Editor's Note: At that time, the full impact of the tragedy had not yet been determined.] We anxiously await the return of peaceful conditions to the lands saturated with blood; then we will know the numbers of the survivors. Now it is our task to help these refugees rebuild their shattered lives. We must sacrifice our time and wealth on their behalf, so that we will remain a united people."

The leaders of the rescue organization quickly recognized this. They formally changed its name to Vaad Hatzalah and Rehabilitation.

Altering a title might signify only word games. The Vaad, though, tackled its new role with a drive born of desperation. Enough Jewish lives had been lost. The survivors had to be preserved–as Jews. Both their physical and spiritual needs had to be addressed, and they had to be transferred to more accommodating climes.

The fundraising continued unabated, and was even intensified. Dr. Samuel Schmidt was again dispatched to Europe, to visit Jews in the Displaced Persons camps and distribute money and basic necessities on behalf of the Vaad. In one D.P. camp in Paris, he encountered eighty young orphans and provided each of them with food and clothing.

"Is there anything else I can get for you?" he asked them earnestly. "Name it, and I'll do my best."

One adolescent boy spoke for the group. "If it's possible, could we have some copies of the *Talmud*?"

When he heard this, Dr. Schmidt knew that whatever he did for these noble souls wouldn't be enough.

Other eminent emissaries of the Vaad included Rabbi Simcha Wasserman (son of Reb Elchanan), Rabbi Solomon Wohlgelernter, Rabbi Zerach Warhaftig, Rabbi Solomon Rosenberg, Charles Ullman and Maurice Enright. Others, like Rabbi Nathan Baruch, Rabbi Avigdor Vorhand and Rabbi Wolf Jacobson set up full-time offices in various locations on the continent. There they toiled for the Vaad on a daily basis, trying to secure kosher food, religious articles, and, especially, entry to the United States, Eretz Yisrael and other desired locations for the beleaguered survivors.

Rabbi Silver, of course, played a leading role in supervising this activity and eliciting the funding for it. However, that didn't satisfy him.

These were his people, and he belonged with them. He

had to personally go and tend to their needs.

He reached his decision. He would travel to Europe. Once again, he would become an angel of mercy. The still chaotic post-war conditions overseas didn't deter him. Nervous comments by family and friends that he should perhaps best leave this arduous initiative to younger men (Rabbi Silver was already sixty-four) were stubbornly dismissed.

However, he would not go empty-handed. First, he insisted on taking with him some one hundred thousand dollars (worth several million dollars today) of the Vaad's funds to distribute to the refugees. He also knew that he would likely encounter uncooperative government officials and anti-Jewish hooligans along the way. Therefore, he armed himself with letters of introduction from his friend Senator Taft and from Senator Alben Barkley (soon to be Vice President), and got permission from the United States government to wear an American Army uniform (which would scare off potential troublemakers).

On June 12, 1946, after months of preparation, he set off on his first overseas flight, a grueling excursion that would last for over three months and take him to ten countries and hundreds of thousands of deprived Jews.

Occasionally, with the help of his American contacts, he had the opportunity to meet with VIP's, like Holland's Queen Wilhemina and the leaders of the governments of Poland and Czechoslovakia. Yet, he used these occasions not to bask in their fame and exchange pleasantries but to plead for his forlorn people.

Thus, when he met with the Dutch Queen, he asked for her help in locating Jewish children who had been taken in by Christians and returning them to their families. (The Queen and her government gave a noncommital reply.) Granted an audience by Sir Alan Cunningham, the British High Commissioner for Palestine, he sought an end to England's restrictions on Jewish entry into the Holy Land. And in his meetings with

Polish Premier Edward Osobka-Morawski, Polish President Boleslaw Bierut and Czech Foreign Minister Jan Masaryk, he presented a list of requests, including an easing of Jewish emigration and a revocation of the ban on *shechitah.*

"I am amazed that you're so concerned with slaughtering cattle when we should be discussing the welfare of the Polish Jews," the Premier responded.

"Mark my words," Rabbi Silver told him. "Those who don't allow the Jews to slaughter cattle will eventually come to slaughter the Jews themselves."

The Polish and Czech leaders—especially Masaryk—were sympathetic to his views and promised to seek measures that would aid their country's Jews.

Through the additional initiative of *hatzalah* activist Rabbi Avigdor Vorhand, working with the Vaad, Dr. Griffel and Rabbi Schonfeld, these governments allowed tens of thousands of Jews to escape from Eastern Europe before they fell under Communist control.

Nevertheless, Rabbi Silver's prime concern was in associating not with dignitaries but with the average Jew. Throughout the trip—in Belgium, in France, in Czechoslovakia, in Italy, and in all the other countries he visited—it was the simple, impoverished Jew whom he sought out.

In some instances, he was pleasantly surprised by what he saw. In Antwerp, Belgium, for instance, he was impressed by the revival of *Yiddishkeit* stimulated by the *rabbanim* and *yeshivah leit* centered there. And in Eretz Yisrael, he was overjoyed to tour the developing *yeshivos* there and to participate in the dedication of a new Bais Yaakov.

More often, though, he encountered survivors who were deprived, depressed, frightened and estranged from Judaism. It was among these people that his aid proved indispensible.

In many cases, what he saw appalled him. When he arrived in Warsaw, Poland, he encountered Torah scholars begging for charity in the streets; in one D.P. camp he saw Jewish youngsters scrounging through the garbage for bread crumbs. His telegrams home conveyed his anguish: "Found terrible situations . . . *talmidei chachamim* lying in streets and living in unsanitary conditions . . . Everyone naked, poor and heartbroken . . . Very discouraging . . . Great work must be done immediately to help Jews in Poland and other countries and bring youth back to Torah . . ."

He sought to undertake that "great work" himself. Wherever he went, he extended whatever aid he could to the needy—the funds he had taken with him, the religious articles he had brought, *talleisim, tefillin, mezuzos,* even the very shirt off his back. As his colleague Dr. Isaac Lewin later recalled, "There were innumerable occasions when, to alleviate the daily needs of the unfortunates he visited, he gave away everything he had on his person without any reckoning."

Very quickly, the one hundred thousand dollars he had brought with him ran out, and he was forced to seek immediate additional funds. He wired back to his Vaad Hatzalah co-workers, "If you do not send help immediately, the whole rescue work will break down . . . I will borrow great sums because I cannot see Jews dying before my eyes."

In fact, he borrowed whatever he could. Every time he encountered a Jew with some financial means, he pressed him for a loan and wrote out his personal I.O.U. to repay him as soon as he returned to America. The sums reached staggering proportions, but Rabbi Silver didn't think twice about the consequences. The money was needed now; how to make good on the loans could be taken care of later.

The debts hounded him for the rest of his life. During the next two decades, Jews would arrive in the United States carrying promissory notes signed by Rabbi Silver and bearing his personal guarantee. Rabbi Silver insisted on making good on every note and every loan. This led to the need for him to borrow additional sums, and his life insurance was mortgaged again and again as collateral for the the loans he made. Somehow, every debt was repaid. However, when he died, Rabbi Silver had hardly a cent to his name.

Nevertheless, he never doubted for a second that he had done the right—and only possible—thing. To Rabbi Silver, money was not something to hoard and squirrel away. It was to be put to immediate use, to alleviate suffering and promote good deeds. (His congregation in Cincinnati knew of his tendency to contribute beyond his means. Therefore, when he was given a monetary award at a *shul* dinner in his honor, the members put the money in trust with an officer of the synagogue. They were afraid that otherwise he would give every last penny away to charity and that his personal needs would go unmet.)

This generosity led to very concrete results. Suddenly, the survivors in the D.P. camps and in devastated Jewish communities were once again able to get food from kosher kitchens, pray with *tallis* and *tefillin* and make use of *mikvaos* as they had once done. They could stop worrying about where to obtain proper clothing or tomorrow's meal and regain a vestige of human dignity.

And there was more. For Rabbi Silver brought not only tangible goods, but—just as importantly—the noble spirit of Jewish concern and the reminder of a religion that still survived. He conveyed this through his acts of *chessed*, his Torah lectures, his empathetic talks and his very presence.

Thus, when he arrived by train in Lodz, a once vibrant center of *Yiddishkeit* that the Nazis had turned into a wretched ghetto, he heard shouts from a crowd milling about outside the station. At first, he feared that the local ruffians had come to harass him. But quickly it became obvious that the welcome was a warm one: These were fellow Jews who had come to greet him. The Vaad had worked tirelessly on their behalf, and they now had a chance to express their gratitute to one of its leaders in person. Lining the streets as he passed, they cheered him and were in turn cheered themselves. The sight of an authentic Torah scholar, regally dressed in a United States Army uniform no less, tapped the pride that had lain buried deep within them for so long.

That renewed pride bestirred a new interest in Torah study, and Rabbi Silver did everything possible to encourage it. In Czechoslovakia, he delivered learned sermons in the legendary Altneuschul synagogue, and in Lodz he invited the populace to attend *shiurim*. In Italy, he announced that he would give fifty dollars to anyone who demonstrated that he had completed the study of twenty-five *blatt* of *Gemara*.

One young man approached him. "I am afraid I never had the opportunity to learn *Talmud* during my life. However, I do know twenty-five *perakim* of *Tehillim*. Is that all right?"

Rabbi Silver tearfully embraced him and made sure that he, too, received the reward.

In Czechoslovakia, he met a small contingent of survivors from the Telshe Yeshivah. Overjoyed, he promoted their continued *hasmadah* and put them in touch with their former *rosh yeshivah* Rabbi Eliyahu Meir Bloch, who had reestablished the *yeshivah* in Cleveland, Ohio.

Wherever he went, he instilled in the dispersed Jews a fresh sense of hope. "His coming to see us made us realize that there was still a future for us as part of the Jewish people," one rabbi later recalled. "He inspired us to overlook our wounds and look forward to better days ahead."

Occasionally, he solved specific problems by forcefully interceding with authorities on the refugees' behalf. For instance, after he saw the youngsters in the D.P. camps sifting through the garbage for food, he stormed over to the local office of the UNRRA (United Nations Relief and Rehabilitation Administration), which supervised the camps. Rabbi Silver did not mince words.

"I am thoroughly shocked by what I've seen here today,"

he told the officer in charge. "You have pity on the local Germans in the area and give them all the food they need, and yet these poor Jews who have known nothing but suffering during the war have to search for a piece of bread. I demand that you improve the situation immediately!"

Then came the incident of the arrested *chassan*.

One camp inmate found cause at last for celebration. He was to be married to a Jewish woman he had met recently. When they heard the news, some good-natured camp supervisors decided to promote the festivities. They knew that alcoholic beverages were extremely hard to obtain, so they gave the man one of their own bottles of wine for use during the wedding rites. The appreciative bridegroom-to-be left them on cloud nine and headed back to his camp barracks. Suddenly, an American soldier patrolling the area stopped him.

"I'm sorry, but you are under arrest," he told the Jew.

The man was flabbergasted. "But why?"

"For being in possession of an illegal item." He nodded towards the bottle in the man's hand. "The liquor. It's against the law for camp inmates to own any."

The flustered man began trying to explain what had happened, but to no avail. He was taken into custody, and the marriage had to be canceled.

As soon as he was alerted to the news, Rabbi Silver acted. Using his diplomatic contacts, he pulled the right strings and had the man released. Then he attended as special guest of honor when the marriage was finally held—and the incriminating wine was joyously disposed of.

Occasionally, Rabbi Silver's own safety became an issue. In Pressburg (Bratislava), Czechoslovakia, he and a fellow rabbi were walking in the street and reviewing a Torah discourse when a gentile suddenly darted towards him menacingly. With hatred contorting his face, he shouted, "I'm going to have you arrested, you filthy Jew. You're speaking a foreign language—it sounded like Yiddish to me, and that's illegal. All you Yids should be in jail anyway."

Rabbi Silver stared straight back at him. "Well, we'll see what my good friend the American consul has to say about that!"

At the mention of the word "American," the man drew back and then scurried off. He didn't mind squaring off against the defenseless Jews, but he wasn't going to take on the Allied army.

Sometimes, though, it was the Americans who caused the problem.

Except for *Shabbos*, Rabbi Silver wore his army uniform at all times. Once, seeing Rabbi Silver advancing towards him in this outfit, a soldier saluted him, as he would any officer. However, Rabbi Silver, in a hurry and preoccupied with his thoughts, failed to return the salute.

The soldier thought this odd. Perhaps this elderly man wasn't a soldier after all. Clearly, with that beard of his, he didn't exactly *look* like a general. The soldier caught up with him and demanded to see his military identification.

Rabbi Silver became agitated. He didn't have any time to waste on this intrusion.

"I don't need any identification papers," he insisted. "I am here on an important mission. I am the Chief Rabbi of the United States!"

The soldier looked at him. "Sure. And I'm General Eisenhower."

"No, I'll prove it to you!" Rabbi Silver pointed to a nearby telephone. "Go ahead. You've heard of Senator Taft of Ohio, right? Just call him up, and tell him Silver is here. He'll back me up!"

The soldier was amused—what did this old man have to do with the powerful Senator?—but he decided to follow through. He contacted his superior officer, who placed the phone call to Taft's office in Washington. After a long delay, the Senator himself was reached. As soon as he heard what had happened, he broke into laughter.

"Yes, that's right," he said. "Rabbi Silver is a good friend of mine. And you'd better let him go quickly. Otherwise, the way he runs things, he'll be issuing orders to all of you there before you know what hit you."

A much more serious incident occurred while Rabbi Silver was in Katowitz, Poland. Informed that the Prime Minister had agreed to meet with him, Rabbi Silver went to the station and was about to board a train. Suddenly, he noticed a horde of Polish peasants crowding around him, pointing to his beard and shouting insults. One of them made a fist and started advancing.

Rabbi Silver didn't flinch. He lifted his head high and, in a commanding voice, warned the crowd to move back, for he was about to see the Prime Minister.

The strange sight of this rabbi in an American army uniform talking in English and mentioning their Prime Minister's name confused the crowd. They were further cowed by his dignified manner and his defiant demeanor. Slowly, they withdrew and sought out other targets.

Rabbi Silver got into the train and continued on his way in safety. When he reached Warsaw, he learned that a pogrom had broken out that previous day, July 4, 1946, in nearby Kielce. Some forty-two Jewish survivors of the Holocaust had been murdered by Polish mobs, and hundreds of others— including dozens of policemen—had been injured. Rabbi Silver referred to the horrible incident in his discussions with the Polish leaders, saying it showed the urgent need for the Jews to leave Poland as soon as possible.

Rabbi Silver's journey ended in Eretz Yisrael, where he met with many Torah luminaries, including the Gerer Rebbe (Rabbi Avraham Mordechai Alter), the Chazon Ish (Rabbi Avraham Yeshayahu Karelitz) and the Brisker Rav (Rabbi Yitzchak Zev Soloveitchik). Then he flew back to the United

States aboard a military plane, landing in Springfield, Massachusetts, on September 16, 1946.

The trip had taken its toll. Not only was he many thousands of dollars in debt, but he had lost thirty-five pounds. (One acquaintance who saw him in Europe commented that he was "living not on food, but on Torah and will power.")

Nevertheless, it had been a supreme highlight of his life and the lives of those he had met and helped. He came home empty-handed, but he had left behind hundreds of thousands of dollars of food and religious articles and priceless doses of renewed hope and faith.

A RICH LEGACY

The work of the Vaad Hatzalah continued for several years after the war. Slowly, steadily, the displaced Jews were brought to safer environments and began reconstructing their lives. Many problems persisted; many young Jews remained lost in Christian homes, for instance. But the Vaad's valiant efforts had an enormous effect on the revival of Judaism, and especially Orthodoxy, after the Holocaust.

Rabbi Silver remained his typically active self throughout these post-war years. He continued to play a major role in the Orthodox world, both through his efforts on behalf of Agudath Israel and Agudath Harabbanim and in his individual initiatives. He still impulsively gave away funds, such as when worthy *rabbanim* asked him to sponsor the publication of their Torah writings. Rabbi Silver was also approached to help build a new *yeshivah* for advanced *talmidim* in Bnei Brak. He was so impressed with the concept that he immediately borrowed fifty thousand dollars and donated it to the project. This contribution kept the dream alive, and soon after the Ponevezh Yeshivah opened its doors.

In his later years, Rabbi Silver was viewed as a revered

elder stateman on the Orthodox Jewish scene. He became a bridge between the *yeshivah* world, led by his friend and colleague Rabbi Aharon Kotler, and the American rabbinate, to which he devoted his life for some sixty years. It was therefore fitting that, when he became enfeebled by old age, the Telshe Yeshivah of Cleveland sent one of their *roshei yeshivah* to visit him every month and discuss Torah issues. These encounters provided Rabbi Silver with immense joy, because they allowed him to continue his primary venture in life—the study of Torah.

Rabbi Eliezer Silver passed away in Cincinnati on the 9th of *Shevat* (February 7), 1968, two weeks before his eighty-seventh birthday. Among those delivering *hespedim* at his funeral were such giants of the Torah world as Rabbi Moshe Feinstein, Rabbi Shneur Kotler, Rabbi David Lifschitz and Rabbi Mordechai Gifter.

Because of the debts he had incurred, Rabbi Silver's estate was, in terms of financial assets, almost minuscule. However, what he left behind was incalculable. As Dr. Isaac Lewin noted, "The man who had raised and handled millions on behalf of his fellow Jews passed away without a penny in his bank account. Yet the spiritual legacy of rescue he left behind remains one of the most inspiring of that era, and it will always be treasured in the bank account housing good deeds for *Klal Yisrael*."

A PURPOSE IN LIFE

RABBI SHLOMO SCHONFELD

Rabbi Schonfeld was a highly creative and dynamic personality, devising highly "original" rescue schemes as the need arose. His efforts resulted in the rescue of many hundreds of rabbis, teachers and Jewish children from Germany and Austria on the eve of the War.

3 — A PURPOSE IN LIFE

RABBI SHLOMO SCHONFELD

POLAND, 1946. THE WAR WAS FINALLY OVER. YET FOR NINETEEN-
year-old Henya Mintz, the torment of persistent, terrifying
anti-Semitic sentiment was very much a lingering reality.

Along with her fellow young Jewish girls living in the
Agudath Israel-sponsored dormitory in Cracow, she was still
afraid. She was afraid to go out in the street, afraid to confront
the bullies who hounded them in public, taunting them with
shouts of, "Hitler should have finished all of you off!"

The other night, someone had hurled a rock through
their dorm window. No one had been hurt, but the shock had
penetrated their very being. The broken glass had summoned
up Henya's own shattered life, and the shards of the last few
nightmarish years had come slicing through her memory,
driving her to despair.

She again relived those horrible moments, the separation from her parents, brothers and sisters—all dead now. The
months of hiding out and just barely avoiding detection. The
brief happiness of living with a *Chassidic* family, and the

heartbreak when that family had moved on. And now, the insecure existence in the dormitory, once again never fully sure if the next day might bring disaster.

She had to get out, she knew. She had to leave Poland for somewhere safe, somewhere she could be a Jew without being persecuted for it. But what would be her lifeline to freedom?

That morning, escape was the dominant theme in all the dorm members' minds.

"I just wish there were some magical road leading out of this country," one girl said wistfully.

"So do I," another chimed in. "But how are we ever going to leave Poland when we don't have any visas or contacts?"

"I wonder if that rabbi from England can do anything," a girl named Gitty said.

Henya turned sharply to face Gitty. "What rabbi from England?"

"Rabbi Schonberg or something like that. He came here from London to help people get out of Poland. Someone just told me about it."

"He came all the way from London to Cracow, just to help Jews leave the country?" Henya couldn't believe this wish-come-true. "Well, why are we sitting around here doing nothing? Let's go see where this rabbi is!"

She made inquiries and found out that his name was Rabbi Shlomo Schonfeld and that he was staying in a Cracow hotel. Together with her friend Chana she went there, only to find a long line of other Jews also hoping to meet with the visitor. They took a seat in the hotel lobby and waited throughout the morning and afternoon. As night settled in, the discouraged girls decided to leave and try again the next day.

As they descended the steps of the hotel, they noticed a statuesque man with a van dyke beard, dressed in a resplendant army uniform and looking very much like what she imagined a *malach* (angel) to be. The man noticed their stares and smiled.

Speaking in Yiddish, he said, "My name is Schonfeld. Were you girls waiting for me?"

"We've been here since morning," Henya replied. "We need your help."

"I'm sorry to have kept you waiting. I've been at one meeting after another. But if you're not too tired, I'll be most happy to see you now. Let's go into the hotel."

As soon as the crowd of Jews saw the rabbi enter, they swarmed around him, presenting their plights. He calmed them and assured them that he would be pleased to meet with each one—after he had first assisted the young ladies.

He escorted the latter to the desk in his hotel room and asked them to sit. "Now, what can I do for you?"

The girls explained that they desperately wanted to leave Poland and that they'd heard that the rabbi could help them do so.

"I can certainly try. Are both of you orphans?"

They nodded solemnly.

"That makes it all the more urgent that you leave," he said. "You need to be with Jewish families again, with your people, living in safety. With Hashem's help, I've been able to bring transports of orphans to England. Maybe I can include you in the next one. Are you by chance eighteen-years-old or younger?"

The girls' faces turned ashen. Chana was twenty, and Henya a year younger.

"Don't worry," he reassured them. "As of now, you're both eighteen-years-old. Now, let me take down your names and some other information, and then I'll apply for visas for you and get you a sponsor. Once all that is taken care of, I'll send a telegram for you to report to the British Consulate in Warsaw." He smiled at both of them warmly. "Hold on for a few more days. You've survived so far. Hashem will see you through this, too."

The girls left the hotel in a buoyant mood, but natural doubt still nagged at them. After so many horrid experiences, could something really be going right?

The answer wasn't long in coming.

Two weeks later, the girls were summoned to the British Consulate. The presiding official asked them to be seated, glanced at their papers and looked them over carefully.

"I have your visas here, but I'm wondering," he said. "You girls are supposed to be eighteen, but you look older. You're not lying to us, are you?"

The girls were stunned. Were all their hopes about to be dashed?

Henya bit her lip and then plunged into fervent protest. "But when we came to him, Rabbi Schonfeld said that . . . "

The official stopped her. "Did you say Rabbi Schonfeld? Are you with his group?"

Both girls nodded.

"I see. Well, in that case, I'm sure everything is in order. Rabbi Schonfeld always knows what he's doing."

From that point on, their papers were processed without any further problems.

Soon the girls received word that the transport was about to depart. The youngsters who formed the group were taken from Cracow to Gdansk by small planes, which held twenty youngsters each. When they touched down, Henya recognized a familiar face at the airport.

"*Shalom aleichem!* Welcome, my children!" Rabbi Schonfeld smiled comfortingly. "I'm glad you arrived safely. From here we go to our boat, and that will take us to England."

Their traumatic life in Poland had indeed come to an end.

The group—all one hundred and fifty of them—boarded the ship, and they cast off for the British coast. It was a bittersweet moment, as the youngsters left behind them the only homeland they had known—a land replete with images of family and friends, but also torment and treachery—to sail forth towards the mysterious future.

Rabbi Schonfeld saw the uncertainty in their faces, the suspicion in their eyes. As the only adult on board, it was his task to cope with their constant need for reassurance and tenderness. There were other problems, too. A number of the children were from non-religious homes, and they could speak only Polish, not the Yiddish that Rabbi Schonfeld used. To top matters off, the voyage was a singularly rocky one, and many of the youngsters got sick en route.

Despite these irritants, Rabbi Schonfeld remained a calm and cheerful force, the steadying ballast on board ship. He kept telling the young passengers of the wonderful lives they were about to begin and taught them snatches of English to prepare them for their new environment. There were songs and stories as well, and reminders of religious lore that they had last heard so long ago, if ever. Slowly, the mood on the ship began to shift, as the youngsters shook off their numbness and gained an air of optimism. For if this valiant and fearless rabbi was any indication of the type of people awaiting them in England, then perhaps humanity wasn't hopeless after all.

The transport landed in England on March 27, 1946. The children were taken to a spacious building and served a sumptuous dinner, the type they hadn't dared dreamed of in Poland. Then towels and toothbrushes were distributed, as well as boxes of new clothing. Nurses were on hand to tend to their individual needs. The youngsters settled down to the sweet sensation of sleeping in their very own comfortable, comforting beds.

As they started growing accustomed to their new accomodations, Rabbi Schonfeld visited each of the youngsters to check on their progress. One of the first he saw was Henya.

"Are things going well for you here?"

"Better than I ever dreamed possible. Thank you, Rabbi."

"You know that in a while our next transport will be coming, with G-d's help. Until then, you're more than welcome to stay here. Is there anyone you could board with afterwards? Any relatives you could go to?"

Henya sighed. "Most of them were killed in the war. There's hardly anyone left, except an uncle in Eretz Yisrael, I think. But I don't know his exact address."

"If you tell me his name, we'll try to contact him," Rabbi Schonfeld said. "Still, I should warn you that getting into Eretz Yisrael isn't very easy right now. You may have to stay in England for a while."

"That's all right. Some of the other religious girls were talking about staying at the Beth Jacob hostel in London. I can get a job, and I'm sure everything will work out fine."

"Well, if there's ever anything I can do to help, just let me know."

Henya considered for a moment. "Thank you, but . . . well, there *is* one small thing. Something that I'd like to find out."

"Yes, of course."

"I've been wondering, ever since I saw you at the hotel in Cracow. You've been so nice and helpful, taking care of us and giving us everything we need. Every time something goes wrong, you're there to fix it. But I still don't understand. Why are you doing all this for us? After all, we're not even related to you."

Rabbi Schonfeld broke into the strong, reassuring smile she had seen so often. "Permit me to disagree with you, Henya. As far as I'm concerned, we're all part of one big family. What I'm saying is, you are indeed my children, every one of you."

EARLY RESPONSIBILITIES

Shlomo Schonfeld was a child himself when he learned the commitment expected in one's service to *Yiddishkeit*. His father was Rabbi Dr. Victor Schonfeld, a native of Hungary-Austria, who had become *rav* of a small Orthodox *shul* in London before Shlomo's birth. Shlomo was a witness to his father's bold decision to break away from the mildly observant Jewish establishment in England and to help create a true Torah-based Jewish community. Towards that end, Rabbi Dr. Victor Schonfeld established the first Orthodox Jewish day school in London. He also founded an active youth group and aided Jewish refugees after World War I.

Then, when Shlomo was almost eighteen, his father suddenly passed away.

At the funeral, Shlomo delivered a moving *hesped*, recalling what his father had said at his last *Rosh Hashanah* sermon: "What we seek on earth is not just life, but a *purpose* in life." It was to become Shlomo's guiding principle throughout his life.

Until his father's death, Shlomo had been pursuing a career as a lawyer. Now, encouraged by his mother, he changed course. While Rabbi Elie Munk temporarily served as *rav* of his father's *shul*, Shlomo prepared to enter the rabbinate himself. He steeped himself in Torah learning at the renowned *yeshivos* of Nitra and Slobodka, and also completed his university training. (In Nitra, his *rebbe* was Rabbi Michoel Ber Weissmandl, the future rescue activist, with whom he established a warm personal relationship. When Rabbi Weissmandl came to London in 1936, 1937 and 1939, he stayed with Rabbi Schonfeld and helped inspire his student's ventures into rescue work.)

In 1933, Rabbi Shlomo Schonfeld assumed his late father's old position as *rav* of Kehillas Adas Yisrael, and he also became head of the local Jewish day school and the Union of

Orthodox Jewish Congregations of London. He was only twenty-one years old.

Many old-time residents of the community at first dismissed this new Rabbi Schonfeld. They scoffed at the attempts of so young a man to lead his flock along a traditional path. They were sure he would never rise to the challenges. Soon enough, though, they were to discover what a persistent and forceful personality he could be.

NEW PATHWAYS IN CHINUCH

One area to which he devoted his full talents was Jewish education. Until this time, the standard practice in England was for Jewish parents to enroll their children in public school and then send them to an after-hours Hebrew School. This system did not inspire enthusiasm for Jewish studies, for both students and teachers in the Hebrew School were already fatigued from a long day's work and mainly looked forward to dismissal. Torah learning was consigned to the position of an also-ran, at best.

Despite this, the leaders of the British Jewish establishment were quite satisfied with this setup. It met the minimum requirements for Jewish education, without interfering with what they considered the central goal—a solid secular training. On the other hand, they attacked the Schonfelds' Jewish day school as making it hard for youngsters to gain full integration into British society.

Rabbi Schonfeld felt differently. He agreed that secular knowledge could indeed be important and useful, both in one's dealings with society and in one's appreciation of Hashem's wonders. However, he argued that the primary focus of a Jewish child's education should be Torah studies. He disregarded his detractors and expanded on his father's work by building an entire network of Orthodox Jewish schools. This included England's first Jewish secondary (high) school, with Orthodox teachers who could thereby supervise all aspects of their students' *chinuch.*

To achieve his goals, Rabbi Schonfeld had to work hard to win the confidence of not only the Jewish public, but also the British government, whose approval was required for all educational systems. This led to many conferences with public officials, during the course of which his natural charm and forceful manner proved highly effective. Later, many of these same officials would come to Rabbi Schonfeld's aid during his rescue work.

At one point, Rabbi Schonfeld was called upon to justify his schools' credentials before the government's Minister of Education. "It's not that we're against Jewish schools, you know," the man assured him. "However, there is a long list of requirements that your schools must satisfy, and we're not sure that is the case, my dear Rabbi. After all, you Jews have you own way of doing things, don't you?"

Rabbi Schonfeld didn't shy away from the issue. "Yes, we are Jews first and foremost," he said, "and Jews have always been renowned for their scholarship. Jews were able to read and write fluently before a single teacher existed in England. We, at our schools, are continuing that high standard of study. Why, then, shouldn't our schools be considered at least the equal of any other?"

Official certification was granted.

This same willingness to meet challenges head-on, alone if necessary, was to characterize the rescue work that would soon come to dominate his time.

A SUDDEN NEED FOR RABBIS

Rabbi Schonfeld's role models in *hatzalah* work were his sainted father and Rabbi Michoel Ber Weissmandl, his *rebbe* at the Nitra Yeshivah.

In the summer of 1939 (with the support of the Archbishop of Canterbury, who had come to admire his brilliance and deep-seated humanity), Rabbi Weissmandl travelled from Slovakia to England to initiate an ambitious plan. He proposed to transfer two hundred Jewish families from Nitra to Canada (which was part of the British Commonwealth). There they would live in a self-sufficient Jewish farm community, far from the reach of the Nazis. He asked his close colleague Rabbi Schonfeld to help implement the plan. Unfortunately, the outbreak of war scuttled the entire venture.

The need to rescue Jews had become clear to Rabbi Schonfeld even earlier, with the anti-Jewish laws in Germany and the Nazi takeover of Austria in 1938. Suddenly, Jews whose families had been distinguished German and Austrian citizens for centuries became enemies of the state overnight.

Singled out for taunts and beatings by mobs, because they stood out conspicuously, were the religious Jews. It became especially dangerous for rabbis and Torah students to remain in both Germany and Austria. But how were they to get out? Which country would accept them?

Rabbi Schonfeld was determined that they would find a new home in England. This was not a simple matter, though. Like many countries, England had experienced an economic depression during the 1930s, and unemployment was high. Potential immigrants who seemed unlikely to take care of themselves weren't wanted. Furthermore, most Jews didn't want to support an influx of rabbis from the continent. They were satisfied with their relatively low level of *Yiddishkeit* and had no desire to see a sudden flood of "old-fashioned" Talmudic scholars upset the religious status quo.

Certainly, Rabbi Schonfeld considered the learned Jews of Germany and Austria desirable refugees. But how could he convince the British authorities of this?

The solution turned out to be amazingly simple. It was

his special genius to be able to come up with creative solutions to seemingly intractable problems, and this was one such example.

The government might not on its own think that there was a need for additional rabbis in England. However, if the respected Chief Rabbi of Great Britain was to state that more Jewish clergy and ritual directors were necessary, they would take his word for it.

Therefore, Rabbi Schonfeld went to see Rabbi Joseph Hertz, England's Chief Rabbi, and suggest a plan. He would set up an organization, the Chief Rabbi's Religious Emergency Council, which would determine how many spiritual leaders were needed in the country. Once permission was given, the rabbis and teachers would be brought over from other parts of Europe, thus enabling them to elude the Nazis.

Chief Rabbi Hertz was delighted with the idea, and gave it his full sanction. He was also very taken with Rabbi Schonfeld and his princely personality and considered it a great honor when Rabbi Schonfeld became his son-in-law in 1940.

Under the Chief Rabbi's Council's auspices, Rabbi Schonfeld was able to gain admission to England of hundreds of rabbis, teachers and *shochtim*, beginning in 1938. Sometimes, he granted potential immigrants *semichah* or *kabbalah* on the spot, to make sure that specific endangered individuals would be granted entry.

In 1939, Rabbi Schonfeld embarked on another massive intake program. By then, he had begun arranging for children's transports to come to England from Germany and Austria. However, young Jews over the age of sixteen could not legally be included in these groups. Did that mean they would be left behind for the Nazis to dispose of as they saw fit?

Not so. To ensure their survival, Rabbi Schonfeld formulated another plan. He set up a *yeshivah* for older students and then saw to it that it enjoyed full enrollment. Once again using the banner of the Chief Rabbi's Council, he had young Jews

153

aged sixteen and over brought over from throughout the continent to attend the *yeshivah* and thereby save their lives. Eventually, these older students themselves became involved in the rescue campaign. One became Rabbi Schonfeld's trusted secretary, and others used the memory of their own experiences to help newcomers adjust to their new British surroundings.

CHILDREN OF SORROW

Rabbi Schonfeld did not cater solely to rabbinical leaders and senior students, though. Especially dear to his heart were the thousands of Jewish children set adrift from their families by the Nazi conquests. Working to save them became one of his top rescue priorities.

It was a phone call from Mr. Julius Steinfeld, a dedicated leader of Agudath Israel in Vienna, Austria, that prompted Rabbi Schonfeld's first large-scale effort to save Jewish youngsters. Rabbi Schonfeld was already acquainted with Mr. Steinfeld. The two had met in Vienna, where Rabbi Schonfeld had many relatives; he admired Mr. Steinfeld's quiet but effective work on behalf of the *klal.* When he heard Mr. Steinfeld's voice on the phone on November 10, 1938, Rabbi Schonfeld was pleasantly surprised. But this was no social call.

"Have you heard the news?" Mr. Steinfeld asked somberly.

"You mean the terrible riots against the Jews? The radio's reporting that the Nazis are burning *shuls* and attacking Jews all over Germany and Austria. We keep hoping it's all just rumors."

"I'm afraid it's all true, and worse. I don't think there's a single *shul* left unharmed here. And they've been arresting Jews right and left. Hundreds are probably dead."

Rabbi Schonfeld gasped. "*Baruch Dayan Ha'emess.* Is

there anything we can possibly do?"

"That's why I called you. I know you've done some rescue work in the past."

"Well, we've gotten some rabbis and teachers to come here through the Chief Rabbi's Council. I'm pleased that worked out, but I'd like to do more."

"Good. There's no telling what might happen next. Anything is possible now. We've got to get as many Jews out of Austria as as possible, quickly, while there's still a chance. And I'm especially concerned about the children whose parents have been arrested or killed. If they don't find new, safe homes soon, I don't know what will happen to them."

"I'll start working on it immediately."

The children had to be spirited out of Austria. But how? A rescue operation like this required a sizable, coordinated effort, one that would need both government cooperation and much help from the Jewish community. Rabbi Schonfeld convened an urgent meeting of his *shul's* board. Speaking forcefully, he described the children's plight and pushed for an emergency drive to bring them to England. When he concluded, he asked for concrete suggestions.

"You're absolutely correct, Rabbi," one member of his *shul* committee said. "We're all for such a project. But, of course, you should realize that it will require careful preparation. After all, you can't just pick up the children and bring them over like you're taking them out to a picnic. You have to find places for them to stay, and clothes for them to wear, and who knows what. It will all take time, and lots of money."

"Still, Rabbi Schonfeld has a point," another member added. "We can't let those poor children linger in Austria. Naturally, it *will* be expensive, as the gentleman just noted. But we must do our bit for our fellow Jews. So I propose that we pledge our support for the rescue of a specific number of these children. Then we can go out and raise the money to bring them over."

Rabbi Schonfeld was pleased. "I'm so glad you agree. How many do you propose that we sponsor. A hundred? Perhaps more?"

The man cleared his throat. "Come, come, Rabbi. Let's not get carried away, shall we? After all, we hardly have unlimited resources here. What I was thinking about was a smaller number . . . perhaps ten. That would be a nice sum to start out with, wouldn't you agree?"

"But only ten?" Desperately, he sought to offer alternatives. "Couldn't we at least reach middle ground? Say, fifty youngsters?"

The members, though, weren't in a mood to listen. They were doing their part; one shouldn't overreach. They adjourned the meeting and left.

Rabbi Schonfeld sat in his office, slumped in his chair. He couldn't blame his congregants. They were well-meaning and sincerely wanted to help. But they didn't seem to realize the full scope of the problem. Saving ten children would, to be sure, be a great *mitzvah*. However, considering how many Jewish youngsters were in jeopardy, saving ten would be like treating a gaping wound by patting it.

Rabbi Schonfeld had no patience for these slow deliberations. He decided that he himself would have to act—and quickly. By the very next morning, he was already in Vienna to consult with Julius Steinfeld and see what he could personally do to help. As soon as he returned to England, he went to the British Home Office, the government agency supervising immigration. He gained access to an influential official, who was impressed at the sight of this dignified rabbi with tears welling up in his eyes as he described the problem.

"Yes, I've heard about the troubles of the Jews in Austria," the man said soothingly. "But there's really nothing that we in England can do about it, is there?"

"I think there is indeed, and I'd like to try it," Rabbi Schonfeld replied. "These are exceptional times, and we have to take exceptional measures. Therefore, I'm requesting permission to bring three hundred Austrian children to England, in order to save their lives."

The official was taken aback. "That's quite a number, Rabbi. And who, may I ask, will be taking care of them?"

"I will."

"You, Rabbi?" He looked him over. "I don't mean to be rude, but how do you plan to do that? After all, you only have two hands, as far as I can see. And where in the world do you have room for so many youngsters?"

"I'm not alone in this. Others will help. Also, I run a school, and I have two school buildings. The students will soon be away on holiday, so I can house the newcomers there, until we find them permanent homes."

"I should warn you, rabbi, that we have strict rules about proper housing for immigrants. You can't just dump them anywhere. I want to see these quarters for myself."

"Be my guest, please."

Rabbi Schonfeld escorted the official to his *yeshivah*, where students were about to be dismissed for *Chanukah* vacation. While classes proceeded, the man measured the exact size of the rooms. Then Rabbi Schonfeld invited him to his office.

"All right, rabbi, I'll concede. You do have plenty of room here. But we can't count the big area below. That has to be used as a dining room. So that means that you really have room for only two hundred and sixty youngsters, not three hundred."

Rabbi Schonfeld considered, and then brought the man to a private house right nearby. "Look at this space. You could easily fit forty children in here."

"So it seems," said the man. "And what do you usually use this place for?"

"Well, I live here," Rabbi Schonfeld said.

"But where will you stay, then?"

157

"No problem," he said. "Up there." Rabbi Schonfeld led the man to a cramped attic. He pushed aside assorted papers and antiques to reveal an old cot. "This is good enough for me, especially when you consider that some of these children haven't had a decent sleep in weeks, and I've had a comfortable bed all along."

The man stared at him in wonder. Finally, in a soft voice, he spoke. "Yes. Yes, I think that if anyone is fit to take care of these youngsters, it's you."

AWAITING THE NEW ARRIVALS

The next step was ascertaining the names of those children who would be coming. For this, Rabbi Schonfeld relied on Julius Steinfeld and other Orthodox Jewish leaders in Vienna, who assembled lists of needy youngsters for him. Rabbi Schonfeld rushed the information to the British Home Office, and an employee there was charged with filling out the passport applications for each child. The work was complex and tedious, and the employee had not quite completed it by closing time.

"Can you come back tomorrow?" he asked Rabbi Schonfeld.

"Yes, but I can also stay late, if you can. After all, if we delay, there's no telling what the Nazis can do in the meantime. Any waste of time could cost the children their lives."

The man understood and put in the extra time until all the papers had been properly filed.

Other preparations kept pace with the paperwork. Beds and blankets had to be secured and additional cooking facilities set up. Local volunteers, including dozens of his day school students and members of the neighborhood Jewish Boy Scout troop, were of immeasurable help during this time, and the arrangements proceeded smoothly.

However, another obstacle soon arose—the weather. Without warning, the worst snowstorm in almost a decade blitzed London. The school that had been so meticulously refurnished to house the newcomers was now snowed in. Yet even that didn't deter Rabbi Schonfeld and his small but loyal crew of students. They grabbed shovels and cleared the way so that the trucks bearing the children could get through. That done, Rabbi Schonfeld rushed to the port of Harwich to greet the youngsters as they arrived at the dock.

One by one, they moved slowly down the gangplank to stare at their new country. Once the children of well-to-do Orthodox families, now frightened, hungry and weak, they clung to each other for support. But they were alive and shyly ready to inch towards new lives.

Rabbi Schonfeld gave them a rousing welcome and helped them onto the trucks that led them to the school. There, neighbors and volunteers were braving the cold to greet them. The children were fed, washed and prepared for a good night's sleep. At all times, Rabbi Schonfeld was in the forefront of the activity, though by now he was dangerously close to exhaustion.

Finally, all the children were taken care of. Rabbi Schonfeld smiled despite the numbing fatigue that gripped his body. The cozy cot in the attic awaited him, but he insisted on making one last tour of the room. All seemed tranquil, until he heard the muffled sobs of one six-year-old, crying in the dark. Going over, he heard her calling for her mother. Tenderly, he took the girl in his arms and soothed her with a lullabye. Only after she was asleep did he finally gain some rest himself.

THE NUMBERS GROW

Rest proved to be a rare commodity for Rabbi Schonfeld. With his limitless energy, he kept going day after day. One transport had been accommodated, but another was soon on its way. At the same time, he had to supervise the running of his *yeshivah* and his *shul*, as well as contribute to community services. It was fortunate that he was an athletic and energetic individual, because he quickly had to adjust to regular twenty-hour workdays. Whenever a sudden crisis arose, he recruited the help of others to deal with the situation.

One Friday afternoon, Rabbi Schonfeld's *yeshivah* high school students were about to return home after dismissal, when Rabbi Schonfeld's car came roaring towards the *yeshivah* building. It came to an abrupt halt, and the rabbi hopped out. "Don't anyone leave!" he shouted. "I need all of you in my office immediately!"

Caught up in his sense of urgency, the students swiftly followed Rabbi Schonfeld inside. There, he breathlessly explained why he had summoned them. He had just received permission to bring hundreds of additional Jewish children over from Vienna. However, the necessary documents had to be filled out right away, or else the opportunity might vanish.

"Each of you must help me in this," he said. "I need the papers filled out properly, and I must bring them all to the Home Office before *Shabbos*. Don't let me down."

The students realized the monumental importance of their task—how many students, after all, get to be key links in a rescue campaign?—and plunged into the work with becoming maturity. Their free time could wait. Due to their vigorous efforts, the job was indeed completed, but only a half hour before *Shabbos*.

Rabbi Schonfeld peered at the clock and then scooped up all the papers and sprinted to his car. He took off for the Home Office like a man bringing his expectant wife to a hospital. It paid off. He arrived moments before closing time and deposited the precious papers on the appropriate desk. Then, since *Shabbos* had by then begun, he left his car where it was and made the return trip—quite a few miles long—by foot. He arrived home with some painful corns and bunions, but also a feeling of total exhilaration. The next time he met his students, he thanked them profusely for their help.

By the time England went to war, in September, 1939, over one thousand refugees were in the country under Rabbi Schonfeld's sponsorship and care.

Rabbi Schonfeld preferred to keep the campaigns of the Chief Rabbi's Council independent of the establishment Jewish organizations. Many of his older colleagues there questioned his bold approaches. "All these Jews flowing into England will only breed anti-Jewish feelings here," some fretted. Rabbi Schonfeld ignored the criticisms; he couldn't waste time on lengthy debates. However, when anyone threatened to subvert his *hatzalah* drives, he fought back like a lioness protecting her brood.

One well-meaning but insensitive member of Rabbi Schonfeld's rescue committee was dissatisfied at the conditions in which the refugee children were living. The man reported his misgivings to the Home Office, indicating that the youngsters were being kept in dangerously cramped quarters.

Rabbi Schonfeld learned of this and reacted with fury. True, there were a lot of children being accomodated, but they were by no means living in squalor. Such a negative report might prompt the British government to bar any further transports of young Jews to England. He quickly met with officials to undo the damage.

Then he went to his *shul* office for a meeting, which was already under way. Seeing that the man who had made the complaints was present, he dramatically flung open the door, pointed an accusing finger at him, and shouted, "*Moser!* Informer! Out!!"

The man, branded an enemy of his fellow Jews, slunk out in shame, never to return. Then the committee went on with the rescue business at hand.

SMALL AND LARGE NEEDS

Once the immediate needs of the new arrivals were met, concern focused on helping them with long-range adjustment.

There were many difficulties to overcome. The youngsters had to get used to a strange country, with an unfamiliar language and a foreign style of life. Many of them were quite wild at first, being deprived of parental discipline. But the teachers and caretakers under Rabbi Schonfeld's supervision provided them with a delicate balance of tenderness and firm direction, enabling them to feel wanted and cared for.

And then there was always Rabbi Schonfeld himself.

Although he was constantly on the go, occupied with his countless activities, he always seemed to be there when the children needed him. Just through his presence, he provided them with a thrill. They were awed that this distinguished-looking leader would take a personal interest in them.

"He always remembered my name," one of his charges remembered years later. "Even with all the children he had to take care of, he never forgot who I was."

Whenever he appeared at the school, bringing gifts and good cheer, the children flocked around him. And he also made sure to solve their special problems, such as in the case of the homesick girl who got to take a very special car ride.

The chaotic conditions of wartime could cause confusion, especially to an insecure child. One girl who had come over with a transport found that, while the children were being put up with families, she had become separated from her younger brother. Already parted from her parents, she now feared that she had lost her last remaining relative. The girl became hysterical and quieted down only when Rabbi Schonfeld promised to locate the boy. He jumped into his car, drove through a totally unfamiliar stretch of country and made one inquiry after another. At last he found the boy and reunited him with his sister. He had set aside other pressing business to accomplish this, but he considered this matter to be of the utmost importance.

Once the war began, the British government ordered all children residing in the cities to be evacuated to the country-side, where they would be spared the terror of the German bombing "blitzes." This order applied to the children in Rabbi Schonfeld's care as well, so he set up schools for them in Shefford and neighboring towns. The schools were under the day-to-day direction of his colleague Rebbetzin Judith Grunfeld (see chapter five), but Rabbi Schonfeld remained the dean, formulating overall policy and visiting the children whenever his schedule allowed for it. As a result of this care, the children survived the war in good physical, emotional and religious condition.

Many years later, as adults, the members of the children's transports remembered Rabbi Schonfeld's kindness with gratitude. "He never treated us as refugees, as statistics of the war," one said. "To him, we were as precious as his own children."

INTERNED BUT NOT FORGOTTEN

Rabbi Schonfeld's care was not reserved only for the young refugees.

When France fell to the invading German armies in 1940, the British grew greatly concerned. They presumed that they would become Hitler's next targets, and they tightened security in the country considerably. There were fears that German spies might try to infiltrate the country, and so the government ordered that all male refugees from Germany and Austria be rounded up. They were forced to leave their families behind and interned in isolated work camps, such as one on the Isle of Man.

Perhaps there were indeed a few spies among the internees. However, there were also many thousands of innocent Jews in the group who had come to England to escape the Nazi terror. They argued that they were logically the last persons in the world who would want to spy for Hitler. Nevertheless, the government insisted on keeping them separated from the general public and, ironically, grouped together with many pro-Nazi Britons of German descent.

For many Jewish internees who still harbored nightmarish memories of concentration camps, the order to go to the internment camps was shattering (though conditions in the latter were far superior to those in the former). In addition to being separated from their loved ones, the Orthodox Jews among the group faced great difficulty in practicing their religion. There were few provisions available in the camps to enable them to observe *Shabbos* and *kashrus* properly. Through their relatives, they pleaded with the Jewish community to come to their aid.

Rabbi Schonfeld was one of those who did. He made good use of his by-now solid political connections and his leadership of the Chief Rabbi's Religious Emergency Council to ease the internees' plight. With the permission of the authorities, he became the first rabbi to visit the detainees during their confinement. The sight of a rabbinical leader who had taken the time and interest to visit them was comforting in itself. But Rabbi Schonfeld brought them more than simply his own personal greetings. He also came with food and financial aid, and with cherished messages from their families. While in the camps, he helped establish *shuls* and *kosher* kitchens, and provided the men with *siddurim, sefarim* and *tefillin*. And he managed to obtain the release of those who were ill, or those he convinced the authorities were "essential" for work in the Jewish community.

Sometimes his intervention led to truly blessed results. One refugee had been sent to the Isle of Man soon after celebrating his engagement to a young lady in London. The man was fortunate. He held a visa to Cuba, and the authorities were willing to release him from the camp so that he could go there. However, he would leave only with his finacee—but she could accompany him only if they were married. Yet, how could the wedding take place if the prospective bridegroom was in an internment camp and the bride was outside?

Once again, Rabbi Schonfeld found the answer.

He pulled the proper strings and arranged for the young lady to be transported from London to the Isle of Man. There, in front of camp officials and five thousand internees, the man and his fiancee were wedded in a joyous ceremony. Soon after, the newlyweds were on their way to a blissful new life together in freedom.

CREATIVE SCHEMES

While always concerned with the war's impact on individuals, Rabbi Schonfeld's many rescue efforts also extended to the masses.

In January, 1943, at Rabbi Schonfeld's initiative, a distingished non-Jewish legislator introduced a resolution in Parliament to provide protective papers (similar to the Latin American papers used by Montello and the Sternbuchs) to Jews in any land under British control. Such a resolution would have served to show the Nazis that the British government would not let Jews become easy prey.

Some Jewish leaders insisted that Eretz Yisrael be specifically listed as one of the British colonies offering Jews a haven. British officials were adamant in opposing this, out of their concern for Arab reaction. The controversy stalled the resolution's progress, as Jewish groups began to publicly squabble about its merits. In the end, it was shelved, despite the benefits it might have provided. Rabbi Schonfeld was crestfallen; it was a sad irony that the Jews themselves had squandered this opportunity.

Another of Rabbi Schonfeld's bold moves was to seek the purchase of Stranger's Key, a small island in the British West Indies, for ten thousand pounds. His purpose was to use the island as a safe haven for European Jews who wanted to escape the Nazis but had nowhere else to go.

He first broached the plan to British officials in an ingenious manner.

"I'd like to ask you a question," he said to a representative of the British Home Office. "If I wanted to, could I invite anyone I wanted to my home?"

"Certainly," said the official. "After all, a man's home is his castle."

"Would that apply to an island, too?"

"What do you mean?"

"Well, if I bought an island, could I ask anyone in the world to come there?"

"I don't see why not," said the man.

"In that case, if I do purchase an island, why can't I invite Jews from all over the globe to come there as my guests?"

"Why not, indeed! A smashing idea!"

So it seemed. However, this project, too, failed to materialize when other British government agencies were not as accommodating as the Home Office and refused to grant it the necessary approval.

Despite these setbacks, Rabbi Schonfeld did succeed in helping Jewish soldiers fighting for the Allies throughout Europe. His Chief Rabbi's Council sent food packages to the front every two weeks, and *matzos*, *haggados* and wine arrived for the Jewish fighting men in time for *Pesach*.

They were appreciated, but Rabbi Schonfeld wondered if he couldn't do more—perhaps make direct spiritual contact with these men amidst the barrenness of the battlefield. Yet, how could this be done while a tumultuous war was in progress?

After much consideration, he came up with yet another brainstorm. Didn't ambulances travel with the troops? And couldn't a few of them be equipped to serve as traveling mini-synagogues as well? The vision became a reality, and the first of the "ambulance synagogues" were dispatched to service the soldiers in the British war zone (especially in Holland) during the final years of the war.

These unique ambulances carried not only medicine but also a supply of *kosher* foods and religious articles, and war-weary Jewish soldiers could come aboard to pour out their feelings in prayer. Later, as British armies helped liberate Nazi-occupied lands like Belgium and Holland, the vehicles became symbols of renewed *Yiddishkeit* among the Jewish survivors. Not only did they provide these downtrodden Jews with food and medical provisions, but they also brought them the first sight of *talleisim*, *tefillin* and *mezuzos* that they had seen in many a year.

Rabbi Schonfeld also reached out to Jews in the front in other ways.

A Jewish soldier was part of a small British advance party that landed in Normandy on the eve of the Allied invasion there in June, 1944. The men were dispatched to a building in Caen, France, and set up camp day. Then most of the soldiers were assigned elsewhere, leaving the Jewish soldier alone in the building on a Friday evening.

He was guarding the position when he heard a startling knock at the door. A voice called out the pre-arranged password, and the soldier was relieved to see the company's sergeant enter. The Jewish soldier stood at crisp attention.

"Oh, it's you," was the sergeant's reaction. "I was looking for someone to stand on guard tomorrow, but I guess I'll have to search elsewhere. After all, you won't be available."

"What do you mean, sir?"

"Well, I received strict orders not to make you do any work on Saturdays if at all possible. You must really have someone looking out for you back home, don't you?"

Just as he had looked out for the Jewish soldier, so Rabbi Schonfeld felt a responsibility to help the debilitated survivors of the Nazi terror even after the war was over.

REVIVING THE REMNANTS

With Hitler dead and the German armies squelched, the Jews of Europe no longer had to fear the Nazi menace. However, there were still many thousands of survivors, including orphans like Henya Mintz, who had little to look forward to in their homelands. Their families were dead or disbanded, their homes occupied by strangers, their Jewish communities shattered, their safety threatened by local anti-Jewish sentiment. In addition, Communism was coming to dominate Eastern Europe like a spreading curse, eroding all chances for a revival of *Yiddishkeit* there.

Many Jews in the Free World were too busy picking up the pieces of their own post-war lives to pay these survivors much heed. Rabbi Schonfeld was not one of them.

He was well aware of the obstacles he faced in aiding these remnants of a once-towering community. Past experience had alerted him to the fact that some fellow British Jews were leery of letting in a flood of survivors. They feared that these foreigners would lead to all of England's Jews being branded as outsiders. In addition, the governments of the Eastern European countries would have to agree to let their Jews depart, and they would probably not negotiate the matter with a single independent rabbi.

To deal with the second issue, Rabbi Schonfeld arranged for his Chief Rabbi's Council to join forces with a non-Jewish group called COBRA (Council of British Relief Societies Abroad), an organization that enjoyed the strong support of the British government. This allowed the workers of the Chief Rabbi's Council to carry out their efforts under more official auspices. In addition, it enabled them to wear the impressive uniforms of the United Nations Relief Administration, known as UNRRA.

So it was with governmental approval that Rabbi Schonfeld, dressed in a smartly-tailored service uniform, took off for Poland in 1946. The uniform stood him in good stead, for it convinced Polish officials that he commanded influence and respect and should therefore be listened to. It also attracted the attention of some Communist snipers, who found the tall gentleman wearing it an inviting target. (The Communists also opposed his efforts to remove Jewish children from lands that would soon fall under Russian domination. They considered it an insult to claim that the children wouldn't want to live in the coming "Communist paradise.") Twice, they fired shots at him, and once they tried to blow up his jeep. However, Hashem was clearly with him, and he escaped injury each time.

Rabbi Schonfeld didn't let these incidents faze him. After intensive negotiations, he got the Polish government to agree to let three major transports of Jewish orphans, totalling over two thousand youngsters, leave the country in stages. He also arranged for the departure of children from Czechoslovakia and Hungary. Finally, he convinced the British government to let them enter England.

Then he had to cope with one more problem. Where would he put all these youngsters when they arrived?

That was soon taken care of, in Rabbi Schonfeld's own inventive way.

He returned from Poland with his first transport just before *Shabbos Hagadol*. Somehow, he found the time to prepare and deliver his traditional scholarly *Shabbos Hagadol derashah* to his congregation. Then, after Shabbos, he and his assistants went directly to his office, where they began phoning one kosher hotel and inn after another.

"Hello, this is Rabbi Schonfeld of Congregation Adas Yisrael. I have a pleasant surprise for you. You are going to have the privilege of hosting five young Polish war orphans as your guests over *Pesach*. Yes, I know you are fully booked over *Yom Tov*, but I'm sure you'll find space for these charming youngsters. After all, you don't want me to send them back to the ruins of Europe, do you? That's very kind of you. Thank you, and *gut Yom Tov*."

The initial placements were made. Then Rabbi Schonfeld turned for further assistance to those he knew he could definitely count on—the refugees he had helped bring over before the war, who were now establishing family lives of their own. They knew from personal experience what these new refugees were going through. As a result, they were more than willing to serve as temporary foster parents and to provide the special care they needed.

As England recovered from the ravages of war, those rescued by Rabbi Schonfeld made smooth adjustments to Jewish life in their newly adopted country. Many became British citizens, while others eventually moved on to Eretz Yisrael and the United States. One of the latter was Henya Mintz, who managed to contact her uncle and, after spending some time living under his wing in Eretz Yisrael, established a new life in America.

Wherever they were, they did their best to remain in touch with their benefactor. Some requested that Rabbi Schonfeld officiate at their weddings or their sons' *brisim*. Many went on to become prominent leaders of Jewish communities throughout the world, including Rabbi Immanuel Jakobovitz, who was eventually named Chief Rabbi of England and, later, became the first rabbi in history to be given the British title of Lord. Others lived quiet lives as simple observant Jews. However, regardless of their station in life, most shared an enormous sense of gratitude towards the man who had been such a profound influence on them.

REPAYING THE DEBT

Therefore, on the occasion of Rabbi Schonfeld's seventieth birthday, shortly before his death, many of his former charges contributed their recollections to a special volume put together through the initiative of Rebbetzin Grunfeld to honor their mentor. Among those who did so was Henya Mintz, who wrote warmly of all that Rabbi Schonfeld had done for her.

Another refugee who had benefitted from his warm assistance, Mrs. Judith Mannheimer Kallman, wrote:

> I owe more than just my physical survival to Rabbi Schonfeld. Had I stayed in Czechoslovakia, I do not know whether I would have been able to hold on to my Judaism, or even to life itself. I was in desperate need for someone to uphold me and show me the way. It was then that Rabbi Schonfeld came into my life. He gave me that kindness, that love which no one else could have given me at that point, because all the people who had meant most to me were gone. I was totally alone, and I think Rabbi Schonfeld sensed it. He actually gave me the feeling that he was glad to know me.
>
> Whenever he greeted me, I felt as if the sun had begun to shine again for me; that, after all, G-d had been very good. Today I am a mature woman, a proud Jewish woman, the mother of three beautiful children who love their Judaism, and I owe it all to Rabbi Schonfeld.

No matter how crowded his schedule, Rabbi Schonfeld always remembered to provide for the needs of his "children." They, in turn, never forgot him—nor should history forget the valiant efforts of a man who met the crisis of his times by devising brilliant rescue schemes and then selflessly carrying them out, so that precious Jewish lives could be preserved.

THE ISTANBUL CONNECTION

DR. YAAKOV GRIFFEL

Dr. Griffel, an attorney in Poland, became one of the most outstanding Orthodox rescue activists during the Holocaust. Until his passing in 1962, he remained in the leadership of efforts to rescue Jewish children still hidden in gentile homes or Church-related institutions.

4 THE ISTANBUL CONNECTION

DR. YAAKOV GRIFFEL

HE WALKED SLOWLY TO THE DOOR OF THE SIMPLE DWELLING, and then paused.

He had travelled countless miles over the past few years, shuttling from country to country to help save lives. He had risked capture and endured discomforts, encountered frustrations and battled bureaucracy. Yet, few of Yaakov Griffel's trips seemed so crucial as this one.

The brutal war was over. There would be no more direct victims of the Nazis, no more threats of mass murder. Still, there were thousands of living victims huddled throughout Europe—Jews who were displaced and unwanted, Jews alienated from their religion, Jews too young to remember a single *Shabbos seudah*. What of them? Would these survivors, too, be lost to their people, added to Hitler's tally by the apathy of their brothers?

At the same time, how could he go on with this enormously exhausting rescue work? It was taking its toll on him, both physically and emotionally. The endless delays, the petty politics, the near successes that had faded into disappointments—how much more could he stand? Perhaps it was time for some other person or some wealthy organization to assume the task for a while. Maybe they would prove more effective. Or was this all just an excuse to avoid responsibility?

There was one individual who could advise him and help him sort out his priorities. That is why he had come to the town of Bnei Brak in Eretz Yisrael to call on one of the true sages of the time—Rabbi Avraham Yeshayah Karelitz, the Chazon Ish. He'd written to the venerable *rav* before, soliciting his suggestions on various matters. Some things couldn't be confined to writing, though. It was time to see the sage face-to-face.

The Chazon Ish had just completed *Minchah* and was conversing with his fellow worshippers when Dr. Griffel entered. Noticing the visitor, Rabbi Karelitz welcomed him warmly, and Dr. Griffel introduced himself. The sage's greetings grew even more effusive, and his face beamed.

"It is a singular honor to have such a holy individual here," he smiled. "But why are you in Bnei Brak? Why aren't you abroad, in Europe, continuing your urgent work?"

"*Rebbe*, that is exactly why I am here," said Dr. Griffel. "To see if that work should continue."

"I understand. Please come with me to my study, and we will discuss it immediately. I know your time is precious."

Once they were alone, Dr. Griffel proceeded to pour out his anguish. "There are so many Jews still suffering, even after the war, but there's just so little I seem to be able to do. For every Jew I try to get to Eretz Yisrael, there are a million and one problems. The British put up every roadblock imaginable. Even with my law degree I have to search for new legal tactics all the time—and still, I don't always succeed.

"And the children! Those are the most tragic cases of all. So many are still being sheltered by Christian families and being brought up as Christians. They have to be saved, and the

Church is resisting. But even if the children are rescued, they can't stay in Eastern Europe. If they do, they'll be doomed. The Communists will never let them grow up as Jews. The only answer is to bring them here to Eretz Yisrael. But once they are set to emigrate, we lose them anyway. The Zionist authorities won't let them stay religious. They use every trick they can think of to wipe out all traces of *Yiddishkeit* from their hearts. It's the final insult to the memories of their dead parents. Sometimes, I wonder if my efforts are really worth it."

"You don't mean that, Dr. Griffel," said the Chazon Ish. "Look at all you've accomplished so far in your *hatzalah* work. All those wonderful things you've done in Istanbul; all those people to whom you've given life-saving certificates. I have heard much about you from my sources, and they all praise you."

"Thank you, Rebbe. You're being overly kind. But perhaps that's just the problem. Maybe I've begun to take whatever success Hashem has allowed me for granted. How can I have the audacity to think that one single individual like me can do what needs to be done? There are thousands of Jews still in Displaced Persons camps, wasting away. Thousands of Jewish children in Christian homes. Major efforts are needed to save them. That should be the work of a world-wide organization. One little would-be rescuer would just get in the way."

The Chazon Ish smiled. "My dear Dr. Griffel—Reb Yaakov—never underestimate what one single individual can do. What would have happened if Avraham Avinu had given up his solitary quest for Hashem? Where would we be now if Moshe Rabbeinu had declined his mission to lead *Yetzias Mitzrayim*?"

"But surely, Rebbe, you can't compare me to those remarkable leaders."

"Each generation has its own select individuals, fit to meet the challenges of the times. Consider yourself, Reb Yaakov. You have the legal skills and political connections to carry out this holy mission of rescue. Most important of all, you have the proper motivation for the task. You do not want glory or fame. You just want to do what the Torah demands. Otherwise you would have gone to some political journalist with your complaints, instead of coming here."

Dr. Griffel silently let the words sink in.

"I understand your frustrations," the sage went on. "Every leader experiences them. But if you ever have doubts, just come to the *bais midrash*. Come watch just one young refugee pouring his heart out in *tefillah* and Torah learning, because he knows he must also learn for all those Jews who weren't saved as he was. And then you won't wonder if your work has been in vain or if it is over. The answer, Reb Yaakov, most certainly is—no!"

Indeed, it wasn't. Perhaps more so than any of the other rescue leaders profiled in this series, Dr. Yaakov Griffel persisted in his *hatzalah* efforts long after the war had ceased. More than a decade and a half after the Nazis were toppled from power, virtually until the day he passed away, he was still preoccupied with the search for young Jews entrusted to Christians during the war, hoping to reunite them with their Jewish heritage.

TRAGEDY AND ESCAPE

Dr. Yaakov Griffel was unique in numerous ways. He was born to a *Chassidic* family in Poland, and he remained firmly devoted to Torah Judaism throughout his life. At the same time, he was one of the few Orthodox Jews in Poland to receive a doctorate in law. Some of his acquaintances wondered why university training was necessary for someone whose overriding intellectual pursuit remained Torah study. However, his legal knowledge later proved invaluable when he had to haggle with government authorities over issues of rescue. In addition, the image of a traditional Jew possessing a broad familiarity with worldly knowledge greatly impressed the non-Jews he would eventually have to deal with.

Uncertainty pervaded the small town of Boryslaw in East Galicia (then Poland) where Dr. Griffel resided in 1939 with his wife and young children. There was constant talk of war, and rumors that the Nazis were set to strike. Feeling out of touch with the onrushing events, Dr. Griffel called his father-in-law, who lived in the bustling city of Cracow.

"The talk of war is just that—only talk," his father-in-law assured him. "I've just been to Warsaw, and they don't expect the Nazis to do anything soon. The Allies wouldn't allow it."

"Then we're safe where we are?"

"I certainly hope so. Still, with Hitler, you can never be sure. He can proclaim peace one day and attack the next."

"What do you recommend then?" Dr. Griffel asked. "I don't want to take any chances, especially with the children."

"Of course. Then why don't you do this? Send the children to the central part of the country. You're living too close to the border, where the oil fields are. Your town will be a tempting target for the Nazis."

The advice made sense to the Griffel family. A tearful conclusion was reached. Mrs. Griffel and the children would relocate temporarily to central Poland. Dr. Griffel himself would remain behind, wrapping up his affairs and preparing to join them as soon as he could.

The date was August 30, 1939. Two days later, on *Erev Shabbos*, the Nazi blitzkrieg attack began pummeling Poland. Warsaw was besieged and bombarded.

With the desperation of a drowning man, Dr. Griffel grasped at any means of reaching his endangered family. He phoned, he telegraphed, he tried to travel to them himself. No luck. All communications had been severed. In the chaos of the erupting war, his dear ones had been engulfed in the tumult. He longed for a word from his wife, for a smile from his children. But they never came. Then, or ever.

In his vain search for his family, Dr. Griffel crossed Eastern Poland, moving closer and closer to the border. He hesitated before making the last, fateful step across. Maybe there was someone there who had seen his family, who could acknowledge their safety. But no. Nothing. And if he remained, he, too, would likely become a casualty of the fighting. There was no other logical choice. Three days after *Rosh Hashanah*, he fled over the border into Romania.

MAKING CONTACTS

Dr. Griffel remained in Romania for over a year. During that time, he devoted his energies to paving the way for other Jews to escape from Poland as well. Working with Moshe Schreiber and other rescue leaders, he began sending South American passports to Polish Jews, in the hope that these would be their tickets to safety. At the same time, he continued trying to contact his family in Warsaw. The search, however, proved fruitless.

In mid-1940, a pro-Nazi regime led by Ion Antonescu gained control of Romania, and Dr. Griffel was again on the run. Through the contacts he had established, he managed to emigrate to Eretz Yisrael, where he became a legal advisor to the Consolidated Diamond Industries firm. However, his rescue work, instead of lagging, intensified. If he could not save his wife and children, then he could at least help others in similar predicaments.

Joining an organization of Jews in Eretz Yisrael who had relatives in Nazi-occupied lands, he soon became a member of its board. This work led to his making constant trips to Jerusalem for consultations with Jewish leaders and British officials. These contacts would later prove invaluable, when his *hatzalah* work became a full-time venture.

Around this time, a Vaad Hatzalah of the Jewish Agency (not to be confused with the Orthodox organization of a similar name established in the United States) was founded in Eretz Yisrael. It was sponsored by a broad spectrum of Jewish political and religious parties in the Holy Land, ranging from left-wing irreligious members of the Jewish Agency, to the Orthodox Agudath Israel. At the insistence of its Orthodox members, one of the Vaad's main goals was to send aid to Jewish victims of the Nazis and to provide them with a means of escape. To gain closer access to these imperiled Jews, the Vaad established a Council of Rescue, called the Moetza, in Turkey. In that neutral country, the Council could more easily reach out to European Jews. Soon, Turkey became second in importance only to Switzerland as a vital link to oppressed Jews.

In the spring of 1943, leaders of Agudath Israel requested a meeting with Dr. Griffel. "Reb Yaakov, you've no doubt heard of the Vaad Hatzalah's Council in Turkey and the rescue work it does there. We feel that the Council must have on it someone who is sensitive to the special needs of *frum* Jews.

"Now, we've heard of your outstanding work helping Jews in Europe, and we feel that you are our man. We would like to nominate you as our representative on the Council. With your many contacts, and your devotion to *hatzalah*, you could accomplish a great deal."

Dr. Griffel was moved by their suggestion, and also a bit taken aback. "*Rabbosai*, I am humbly grateful for your kind words. But you have to understand that I have never officially belonged to the Agudah, or to any other party. I feel that restricting myself to any one political group would limit my actions. Maybe you would prefer to choose someone with closer ties to your worthy group."

"There is no need, Reb Yaakov. We trust you fully."

Soon after, Dr. Griffel left behind the hallowed hills of Eretz Yisrael for the foreign environment of Turkey.

ISTANBUL ENCOUNTERS

He arrived in Istanbul, the capital of Turkey, shortly after *Pesach*, 1943. There he found that he had been assigned an office of his own, to serve as a site for meetings that might facilitate aid to European Jews. He also met Chaim Barlas, the chairman of the Moetza (the Council of Rescue). Barlas was the head of its Aliya Department, which seemed to make him a natural proponent of European Jewish emigration to the Holy Land.

However, as Dr. Griffel was soon to learn, Barlas was an ardent Socialist Zionist, whose primary concern was paving the way for rugged young Jewish pioneers to make *aliya* and help develop the land, especially in the *kibbutzim*. This did not always square with Dr. Griffel's mission to rescue Jews, including aged and scholarly Orthodox Jews, from Hitler's grasp. In Barlas's eyes, Orthodox Jews were considered "unproductive," since they could not be expected to work the land and develop the country in a physical way. He wasn't interested in the positive spiritual impact they would have on Jewish life there.

Barlas and Griffel clashed frequently over the best method of procuring rescue. For one thing, Barlas was a strict autocrat, who was reluctant to delegate authority. If anything was to be done, he wanted to control it from beginning to end and in this way have final say over who made *aliya*. His approach also showed little sense of urgency towards saving the endangered Jews. He was content to let the organization operate with its customary slow speed, despite the need for swift action. As Dr. Griffel saw it, Barlas was a cold, plodding bureaucrat functioning at a time when Europe's Jews needed a flexible, brotherly advocate.

Dr. Griffel's own view was based on the Torah's instructions that in times of peril anything and everything must be done to save lives. No rescue attempt could be ruled out, even if its likelihood for success was minimal. Barlas rejected such daring in favor of accepted socialist perspective, which considered only an initiative that would probably succeed. It was inevitable that the two men would disagree over priorities.

Some of their fiercest arguments were over the issue of providing trapped Jews with Palestine certificates. Similar certificates from Latin America had already been put to good use by the Sternbuchs and George Mantello (see Volume I, Chapters 4 and 5). Following suit, Dr. Griffel began sending Palestine certificates to those Jews in Europe who requested them. These certificates did not guarantee their holders safe passage to a new country. However, they often did provide protection to those who possessed them. This was partly because the German government feared that maltreating certificate holders would lead to reprisals against the hundreds of thousands of Germans living in other continents, like South America. They would also indicate England's interest in having these Jews enter Eretz Yisrael.

Dr. Griffel showed no hesitation. He threw himself into this activity wholeheartedly. The moment a request came from Europe for an entry visa to Eretz Yisrael, he rushed the information to Jerusalem. He did so by means of cable, instead of the cheaper but painfully slower surface mail service.

This process continued for quite some time. Then the matter of the certificates came up at a Moetza meeting chaired by Barlas.

"We understand that you've been sending messages to Jerusalem by cable, Dr. Griffel," he said. "Is that so?"

"Absolutely correct. I've been relaying requests for Palestinian certificates."

Barlas eyed him with surprise. "My dear Dr. Griffel, I'm sure you know that cables cost a lot more than regular mail. Do you think we're overflowing with money? Besides, this whole idea of saving Jews with certificates is a fantasy. What good are these papers if the British don't let Jews into

Palestine anyway?" Barlas's words grew pointed. "Next time, Griffel, I'd suggest you be a little more careful with our money, and a little more realistic. After all, we can't throw away our funds on plans that don't stand a chance to succeed."

Normally, Dr. Griffel was quite reserved. But now he felt the fury tingling through his body. In an even but sharp voice, he made his reply. "Gentlemen, as long as there exists a post office willing to accept my cables, I will continue forwarding requests for certificates to Jerusalem in the speediest way possible. It is my *duty* to do so as fast as I can; *lives* are at stake! So let me be crystal clear. There is no power in the world—neither political nor financial—that will stop me from doing so." And he proceeded to send additional cables, as before.

Dr. Griffel's sense of urgency concerning the certificates was not shared by British officials, who still held the reins in Eretz Yisrael. When such certificates were issued in Jerusalem, they were not sent directly to Turkey, a process which would have taken only a few days. Instead, they were rerouted to England—at a time when the war had severely slowed mail delivery. As a result, immigration certificates often arrived in Istanbul *half a year* after they had originally been issued. By then, of course, many prospective recipients of these papers already lay in mass graves.

Then, in August, 1943, at the height of the war, England demanded new rules. These further complicated the issuance of these documents.

Until then, the initial request for the certificates required only the name of the head of the family. The names of the other family members could be added later. However, British authorities noticed that Jews sometimes added names of youngsters who were not their own children. This was hardly surprising, since Jews were looking for any means for their families to escape. Those lucky enough to get the certificates were more than willing to take with them someone else's children, so at least they could be saved. But the British were not intent on saving Jewish lives. On the contrary, England saw the desperate Jews as a threat, because they might try to enter Eretz Yisrael. This, in turn, would anger the Arabs, whose oil supplies were vital to British interests.

Therefore, a clamp-down was instituted. From then on, the exact names and ages of each family member had to be listed in all requests for certificates. That way, no names could be added later, and fewer Jews would make it to safety.

Once word of these new regulations spread, Dr. Griffel acted. "We're allowed only a few certificates a week," he told Barlas, "and we have to fill them out immediately. If we don't have the exact information about these applicants on hand, we might lose even these few. We'd better find out the names and ages of all those Jewish families who want papers, and we'd better find it out now, so we won't need to ask for it later, when it's too late."

"You're pushing too hard," Barlas told him. "Why do you get so hysterical all the time? And why do you want to frighten those poor Jews in Europe? They're depressed and tired enough as is. Don't drive them crazy with new paperwork."

Once again, Dr. Griffel disagreed. He wasn't about to take any chances. Defying the Moetza chairman, he hustled to get the necessary data available, just in case it was needed on the spot. The only names he was given were those on a list of religious Jews prepared by Agudath Israel. He therefore wrote to these Jews asking for the pertinent information and received prompt replies.

Some time later, directives came to Istanbul via London. Nine visas would be allotted to Jews each week. The names of those seeking the visas, as well as the names of their dependents and other vital information, were all needed immediately. If the data were not made available right away, the unused visas would be lost forever.

The members of the Moetza were stunned. Where could they obtain this information so quickly?

Dr. Griffel, though, was prepared. For the next several weeks, he was the only member of the Moetza able to provide the essential data for the certificates. As a result, each week nine religious Jewish families from Europe were able to make their way to safety.

Soon word from Zionist leaders in the Holy Land reached the Moetza: "Why are only Orthodox families arriving?"

Dr. Griffel was asked to reply.

"Do you think I'm playing politics here, when lives hang in the balance?" he answered back. "Do you think I ask whether a Jew keeps *Shabbos* and *kashrus* before I allow him to be saved? To me, every Jewish life is dear. And that's why I took no chances about having the family data of European Jews recorded here. If you're unhappy that the only Jews whom I was able to contact were religious, then that is your own fault. Isn't that so, gentlemen?"

For once, Barlas had to admit that Dr. Griffel was right.

YOUNG WOMEN OF VALOR

After the German army occupied Hungary in March, 1944, the opportunity for Hungarian Jews to use visas to Eretz Yisrael grew highly remote. Most of the Moetza members lost all interest in sending any further certificates to Hungary. They dismissed the service as a waste of time. Not so Dr. Griffel.

"Even if Jews can't get to Eretz Yisrael, they can use the papers for protection," he argued. "Look at what Mantello, the Sternbuchs and Chaim Eiss have accomplished. Look at all the lives they've saved by giving out Latin American papers."

"Please, Griffel. Let a Jew talk. Your plan won't work. The certificates might have saved a few lucky Jews over the years, but they're the exceptions. We can't throw away money on wild schemes. These papers won't do any good."

"But if they save even one life—"

"Please! Enough already! Can we move on?"

But Griffel wasn't finished yet. "Here, let me tell you a story. The person who told it to me saw it happen himself. The Nazis were rounding up Jewish families in Poland. No one was being spared. The Jews were told that they were going to labor camps, but the truth was clear. There were tears; there were prayers. The situation was bleak. But for one family, there was a glimmer of hope. They had Latin American papers, and they'd heard that this might offer protection.

"Soon, the Nazis came and demanded that the family join the round-up. The father came up to them. 'But we have these important papers!' he said, waving them in the Nazis' faces.

"Then, in full view of others, the Nazis knocked the papers out of his hand and dragged him and his family away."

Dr. Griffel paused. The others looked at him quizzically.

"So?" one of them said. "The papers didn't help after all, did they?"

"No, not that family," Dr. Griffel admitted. "But someone else who saw what had happened picked up the papers and kept them. Then when the Nazis came to get him and his loved ones, he showed them the documents. 'I have the protection of a foreign country,' he told them. 'If you touch me, you'll wind up in trouble.' And the Nazis left this person unharmed.

"Which is exactly my point," Dr. Griffel concluded. "You never know when the papers might become lifesavers. Even if the papers cost us, don't you think they're worth the trouble?"

Barlas and the others finally relented; Griffel could have his way. However, the issuance of the certificates would be under the juristriction of the Palestine Office in Istanbul, directed by Dr. Joseph Goldin.

By this time, Dr. Griffel had formed a symbiotic partnership with Joseph Klarman, a non-Orthodox representative of the Revisionist Zionist Party. Though he did not observe traditional Jewish practices, Klarman admired Dr. Griffel greatly, describing him as follows: "Griffel was blessed with the character and tolerance of the sage Hillel. Personally most stringent in the observance of Torah, he never hesitated to take any step possible to save a Jew—any Jew."

For his part, Dr. Griffel was heartened by the view of Klarman and his fellow Revisionist Zionists that all European Jews should be rescued for eventual settlement in Eretz Yisrael. This contrasted with the approach of the Socialist Zionists, who wanted only the ideologically-minded *chalutzim*—the hearty secular pioneers—to populate the Holy Land.

Together, Dr. Griffel and Klarman went to see Dr. Goldin, and explained their interest in sending out the certificates. Goldin was sincere in his offer to help. However, both Klarman and Dr. Griffel soon concluded that he just did not have the resources or the drive to mass-produce the papers with dispatch. Who, then, could assist them in their project?

In the end, they relied on the good will of the local Jewish populace.

Through word of mouth, they mobilized a sizable crew of young Jewish women who lived in Istanbul. These young ladies were willing to donate their time and talents to produce and process the papers. Coming to the office that Dr. Griffel had rented for the occasion, they agreed to work past midnight, to assure that the job would be completed accurately and quickly.

Their assignment proved to be notably monotonous. It entailed filling in names and other data on paper after paper and making sure that all the information was completed in the prescribed way. Despite the drudgery involved, the young women took to the task with excitement. They were finally doing something that would, in a way, thwart the hated enemy and provide encouragement to their fellow Jews.

At the job's conclusion, all those involved felt suffused

with a sense of accomplishment. They had succeeded where the Moetza's bureaucracy had failed. And, indeed, the certificates did eventually come in handy. They were shipped by diplomatic courier to Hungary and distributed to the Jews there. Using them, many Jews were able to gain the diplomatic protection of the Swedish Red Cross and the Swiss government.

In all, it was later estimated, several thousand Hungarian Jews were rescued through Griffel's very special initiative.

THE GREAT AND THE POWERFUL

In the course of his rescue work, Dr. Griffel had the opportunity to encounter numerous *gedolim* and governmental VIP's. Instead of turning slack-tongued and goggle-eyed when meeting these personages, he used the occasion to win their enthusiasm for (and, if possible, participation in) the *hatzalah* effort.

The most revered of these distinguished individuals were the *rabbanim*, whom he consulted for advice and *chizuk*. Aside from the Chazon Ish in Eretz Yisrael, Dr. Griffel was in close touch with Rabbi Eliezer Hager, the Vizhnitzer Rebbe, and Rav Zusha Portugal, the Skulener Rebbe. The latter kept Dr. Griffel fully informed of the plight of Romanian Jews. After the war, Dr. Griffel worked hand in hand with the Skulener Rebbe to help young Jewish orphans filter through the Iron Curtain and reach Eretz Yisrael.

Dr. Griffel also maintained close ties with other Orthodox *hatzalah* activists, such as the Sternbuchs, George Mantello and Yisrael Chaim Eis, the outstanding Swiss rescue activist who sent thousands of aid parcels to European Jews. He was also in touch with the Vaad Hatzalah in New York and stood in awe of Rabbi Michoel Ber Weissmandl. Rabbi Weissmandl in turn considered Dr. Griffel a most trustworthy fellow rescue worker. Dr. Griffel was one of the colleagues to whom Rabbi Weissmandl rushed his proposal that the Allies bomb the railroad tracks leading to Auschwitz, with the plea to publicize it in the most effective way possible.

Rabbi Weissmandl's confidence was well-placed. As soon as Dr. Griffel received the impassioned request, he took action. He joined forces with the Agudah activist Lajos Kastner of Slovakia (not to be confused with the Socialist Zionist leader Dr. Rudolf Kastner), who was well-acquainted with the location of the rail lines. The two men traveled to Ankara, Turkey, to meet the American Ambassador Laurence Steinhardt in connection with Rabbi Weissmandl's proposal. Because of the absolute urgency of the issue, they set out on Friday afternoon and reached the Ambassador's office on *Shabbos*, which also happened to be *Erev Shavuos*.

The Ambassador—an assimilated Jew who had been prodded by Orthodox Jews towards greater involvement in rescue work—was eager to receive his visitors. He, too, knew and admired Rabbi Weissmandl and found his plan remarkable. But he pointed out that the implementation of the plan would require Soviet agreement, since the areas to be bombed were located in the Soviet sphere of action.

Both the Ambassador and Dr. Griffel therefore met with Soviet officials about the matter. Dr. Griffel offered to visit Moscow for further discussions. Unfortunately, the Russians never gave him the courtesy of a reply, in regard to this or any other rescue scheme. The matter died there.

Other ventures were more successful. Once the American War Refugee Board (the government agency devoted to rescuing the victims of the Nazis) was established in 1944, Dr. Griffel formed a productive working relationship with its representative Ira Hirschman. Through the good offices of Yaakov Rosenheim and the Vaad Hatzalah, Dr. Griffel was named an official of the War Refugee Board and thus was able to gain invaluable access to the free cable facilities at the

American Embassy in Ankara. In turn, he helped spur the Americans to a growing awareness of the urgent need to aid trapped Jews.

One consequence of this pressure was a major meeting arranged by Ambassador Steinhardt involving Hirschman and the Romanian Ambassador to Turkey, Alexander Cretzianu. Hirschman expressed his concern over the fate of the remaining fifty thousand Romanian Jews then living in Transnistria, once part of Hungary. "We have to do something to rescue those who are left," the American told the Romanian Ambassador. "So many have been killed already; we can't let this tragedy continue."

Cretzianu noticed the American's earnest interest in the issue. "If this means so much to you in the United States," he replied, "then why didn't you come to us about it sooner? If you had, we might have been able to save many additional lives!"

Nevertheless, the Ambassador agreed to help, and he proved true to his word. There were other helpful non-Jews, too. Many were contacted by Rabbi Yitzchak Izak Halevi Herzog, the Ashkenazic Chief Rabbi of Eretz Yisrael. Both Rabbi Herzog and Dr. Griffel met with various Church leaders, including Cardinal Roncalli, the future Pope John XXIII, who was especially sympathetic to their cause. Another influential individual contacted in this way was Queen Mother Helena of Romania.

The upshot was that, in 1944, some five thousand Romanian Jews—including one thousand Jewish orphans—were taken to Eretz Yisrael, thus escaping Nazi subjugation. The bold, "unrealistic" dreams of mass rescue had been realized through the hard labor of Dr. Griffel, Klarman and their dedicated co-workers.

During this time, Dr. Griffel's extraordinary and selfless dedication to rescue manifested itself in an encounter with the Socialist-Zionist members of the Moetza. As an official member of the WRB, his negotiations now had the blessings of the powerful American Government behind him. Among other things, this earned him greater respect and simultaneously won him greater independence from Barlas's narrow *aliya*-focused operations. Without Barlas' knowledge, one of his colleagues on the Moetza, Ehud Avriel, approached Dr. Griffel.

"While we may have our differences," he said, "I know you're an honorable person who can be trusted. I wonder if you could assist us in an important rescue effort."

"By all means. How can I help?"

"I know that the WRB has approved the transfer of a large sum to you from Vaad Hatzalah in New York. Do you think that you could provide us with a loan for a special rescue project I'm working on?"

"I'll certainly make the request. How much do you need?"

"Twenty-five thousand dollars."

This was quite a substantial sum, in fact, the full amount which Vaad Hatzalah had, but Dr. Griffel didn't hem and haw. Instead, he immediately contacted Dr. Joseph Klarman and Ludwig Kastner, his colleagues on Vaad Hatzalah, and they decided to proceed with the loan. It was given without fanfare, and Ehud Avriel was grateful.

In the meantime, Barlas had returned from a trip, fuming at Dr. Griffel. He was angry enough at Griffel's new status with the WRB and Vaad Hatzalah of New York, all of this beyond Barlas's control.

"And furthermore," Barlas raged at the next meeting of the entire Moetza, "I understand that you, Dr. Griffel, have been taking our loans for rescue work without authorization! What exactly is this money going for, and where? I want an answer immediately."

Griffel could easily have turned Barlas into a total fool in front of all his colleagues by revealing that it was Barlas's close friend Ehud Avriel who had come to him for a large loan, and not the reverse. However, Griffel had no intention of embarrassing anyone no matter how strongly he disagreed with him. Instead, he simply said that he would discuss the matter with Barlas in private.

The months passed, and the loan to Avriel was never repaid. Unobtrusively, Dr. Griffel consulted the well-known Torah authority and rescue activist in Eretz Yisrael, Rav Cheskiah Yosef Mishkowsky and asked whether a *din Torah* to reclaim the money was in order.

"Was the money used for rescue?" asked Rav Mishkowsky.

"I believe so."

"Then I don't think you should pursue the issue any further. The funds were put to good use."

Dr. Griffel accepted the *psak* without a murmur, and even though the Zionists never repaid the twenty-five thousand dollar loan, he considered the matter closed.

LOST CHANCES

Sadly, ideological clashes undermined other large-scale salvage schemes.

Plans were afoot to bring large numbers of Hungarian Jews to Eretz Yisrael by boat. One proposed method of doing so was to bring the Jews there via Turkey. This, however, raised the ire of England, which refused to stand up to Arab opposition. The message therefore went out from London to Ankara: "Do not allow one Jew to enter Palestine by way of Turkey!"

The Turks complied, and the Jews were left stranded.

Not all the roadblocks were of non-Jewish origin, though. Thousands of Hungarian Jews, using precious Palestine certificates, managed to stay alive during the war by sneaking across the border to Romania. But they were still in peril, and longed to flee to Eretz Yisrael. However, the Jewish Agency (the Jewish governmental body in Palestine) had control over the limited entry visas to the Holy Land. The Agency leaders parceled out these visas carefully, based on political affiliations. The Agudah had been allotted six percent of the visas. Therefore, no more than six percent of all Orthodox Jewish visa applicants would receive them, whether or not they belonged to the Agudah. As a result, most of the large contingent of about one thousand Orthodox Jews were refused entry.

Dr. Griffel was outraged. "We aren't playing a numbers game here," he fumed. "We're talking about saving priceless lives, not arranging for *aliya*!"

The Vizhnitzer Rebbe, in Bucharest, was likewise furious. "A boat must be chartered to take all these unwanted Jews to Turkey immediately!" he cried.

Agudath Israel and the Vaad Hatzalah applied pressure on the World Jewish Congress and other groups to follow just such a course of action. Chaim Barlas gave his word that he would cooperate.

In the end, though, nothing was done. The Jewish Agency threatened to retaliate against any shipping company that supplied a boat. The Agency wanted to maintain full control over *aliya*, and would not brook any interference with its monopoly, no matter what the cost might be.

No boat arrived. No Jews were saved.

"If only . . ." Dr. Griffel kept lamenting long after the war was over. But such thoughts couldn't, of course, bring back the victims of these petty political feuds.

THE WAR ENDS; THE BATTLE CONTINUES

The Allies were victorious, the Nazis were vanquished, and only then did the world begin to take note of the Jews' massive losses. Sympathy abounded. Unfortunately, it was of no help retroactively.

With his immediate task at an end, Dr. Griffel returned to Eretz Yisrael. It was a chance for him to recoup after the harrowing war years, an opportunity to settle back and enjoy a normal life. Part of his weary self must have longed for some stability and relaxation.

It was the other part of him, though—the part that realized that Jews still needed his help—that proved dominant.

In mid-1945, he was approached by a Rabbinical Rescue Committee in Eretz Yisrael, whose members included such prominent *roshei yeshivah* as Rabbi Yechezkel Sarna, Rabbi Eliezer Yehudah Finkel and Rabbi Isser Zalman Meltzer. Its head was Rabbi Chezkiah Yosef Mishkowsky, a colleague of Rabbi Chaim Ozer Grodzenski and an outstanding writer. The *rabbanim* asked Dr. Griffel to persist in his *hatzalah* efforts. They were all well aware that many thousands of survivors were still languishing in Displaced Persons camps throughout Europe. If these Jews were left to wither away in these depressing dens of despair, still subjected to poor conditions and prejudice against Jews, they would remain victims, cast off from their people. They had to be contacted, uplifted and, if possible, brought to the West or to Eretz Yisrael. The rescue work had to go on.

With the help of Rabbi Herzog's son Yaakov, as well as the Sternbuchs, Dr. Griffel received a visa to return to Europe. Securing permission for this document was far from easy, for the British authorities were suspicious that he might use it to ship illegal arms back to Eretz Yisrael. Nevertheless, in June, 1945, Dr. Griffel received the first visa issued to a Jewish resident of Palestine since the war's end. Immediately afterwards, he was off to Europe.

After meeting with Mrs. Sternbuch in Switzerland, he traveled with her to Germany, where many dispossessed Jews were living in poverty and pondering their future. They briefly visited Camp Feldafing, where the residents still painfully bore the wounds of their concentration camp experiences. Nevertheless, Rabbi Yekusiel Halberstam, the Klausenburger Rebbe, had managed to begin rebuilding a Jewish community there, despite the paucity of religious articles. A kosher kitchen had been established, and Jews began lining up at dawn for the chance of putting on the camp's few pairs of *tefillin*. The visitors offered whatever aid and support they could.

From there, they traveled on to Munich, where the devastation of the war was even clearer. Under the prevailing conditions, with people scrounging for a living in the bombed-out ruins of a once-thriving city, little religious revitalization had occurred. The future looked distinctly grim for the survivors there.

Soon after Dr. Griffel's arrival, he was approached by a group of concentration camp survivors in the city. "We hear you have come from Eretz Yisrael. Can you help us?"

Dr. Griffel looked at the bedraggled group, and his sense of inadequacy was never stronger. "Of course, my dear friends. I'll do anything I can, anything. But . . . I'm afraid I must tell you that it won't be easy. Because of the war, everything is so scarce. Getting money, getting visas—it's all so hard. Still, you deserve the world. I'll do my very best."

"Maybe you didn't understand," said their spokesman. "We wanted you to organize a *minyan* here for *Shabbos*. We haven't had one since the war ended."

Dr. Griffel was moved beyond words. "Of course," he murmured. "You will have your *minyan*. Everything will be taken care of. That is the very least I can do."

"Thank you for all you're doing for us," they said.

"It is I who have to thank you," he replied. "You are the ones who are providing *me* with *chizuk*."

After all they had gone through, he mused afterwards, it was remarkable that holding a *minyan* was their top priority.

That *Erev Shabbos*, he led a group of ragged but unbowed Jews in the *Shabbos tefillos*. Most of them had forgotten their Hebrew, or had never learned it. Many had no hats or caps and had to cover their heads with handkerchiefs. Yet, they prayed as only they who had known hell could, with a fervor hardly matched in the holiest of *shuls* anywhere.

"The emotional level of these Friday night services cannot be described in words," Dr. Griffel later wrote. He resolved to do whatever he could for Jews like these, whose spiritual glow might have been dimmed but certainly not extinguished.

AIDING THE REFUGEES

From then on, until his death in 1962, Dr. Griffel worked without rest to aid the survivors in any manner possible.

This assistance took a variety of forms. It meant meeting the survivors' physical and religious needs in their temporary shelters, as they recuperated from the trauma of their experiences. And it meant finding them new homes, where they could once again seek out their battered identities as proud and loyal Jews.

In the D.P. camps he visited, Dr. Griffel worked hard to ensure that the inmates' requests for religious articles were met. This often brought resistance from those running the camps, and even from Jewish organizations.

In Italy, he was asked to arrange for the delivery of kosher food for *Pesach*. Even the many Jews who had gotten used to eating non-kosher food during the war wanted to partake of this return to tradition. However, the officials for the Joint Distribution Committee, in charge of food distribution, balked. "It would cost too much money," they claimed. Instead, only those who had asked for kosher food earlier would be allowed it now.

Dr. Griffel's arguments made no impression on them. In the meanwhile, the Jews in the camp were threatening to set fire to the kitchens if they were not provided with kosher food.

Looking for assistance, Dr. Griffel wrote a long letter to Rabbi Joseph Schneerson, the Lubavitcher Rebbe (father-in-law of the present Lubavitcher Rebbe), who resided in Brooklyn. Rabbi Schneerson was partially paralyzed and in generally poor health, but Dr. Griffel hoped he could somehow resolve the problem.

A few days later, a phone call came from the United States Embassy to those running the camp. Its message: "Supply kosher food to anyone who wants it, whether he asked for it before or not."

The order was followed, and from then on, the camp residents had no problems with *kashrus*.

Dr. Griffel never learned how the ailing *rebbe* had managed to get the heads of the Joint Distribution Committee to change their policy. Nevertheless, his intervention had worked.

Dr. Griffel himself managed to establish solid working relationships with Jewish organizational leaders who played major roles in forming camp policies. Many were non-religious, but he helped bring them to an appreciation of the needs of the Orthodox inmates. Most proved sympathetic in the end.

When one such leader, Abraham Shereshevsky, wanted to reduce funding for the upkeep of kosher kitchens, Dr. Griffel asked to meet with him.

"Don't you see how important it is to these people to keep kosher?" he asked Shereshevsky. "After all these years when the Nazis mocked Judaism and beat them for keeping *mitzvos*, they can finally practice their religion again. And now, because you're a few dollars short, you're going to deny it to them again?"

"Personally, I don't understand all these religious needs," Shereshevsky replied. "I'm not religious in any way myself, you know."

"Then let me ask you this, Abraham. If you were the head of the Jewish Agency, and you had the power to abolish religion, would you do it?"

Without hesitation, Shereshevsky answered, "No."

Dr. Griffel remained silent, and let the answer sink in. "But why not?" he finally asked. "If you're so opposed to religion, why wouldn't you just get rid of it?"

Shereshevsky said nothing.

"I'll tell you why you said no," Dr. Griffel said. "That wasn't your logical mind speaking. No, that was the voice of your ancestors, the voice of the eternal Jewish spark within you. It was your better inclination, the part of you still dedicated to the traditions of your people. I ask you, then, how can you prevent these people, who have gone through so much suffering, from keeping these traditions?"

The funding for kosher food remained intact.

Despite all these accomplishments, Dr. Griffel realized that helping Jews in the camps was only a temporary solution. They had to be helped back to their feet, but then they had to be led elsewhere. They could no longer stay in Germany, or in Eastern Europe, where anti-Jewish sentiment still smoldered. With the Communists taking over country after country, Jews under their domain would again be trapped. Even if they would not be killed, they would still be prevented from practicing their religion freely.

Therefore, together with others, including the Skulener Rebbe and Rabbi Avigdor Vorhand of Prague, he worked hard to resettle as many Jews as possible in Eretz Yisrael or America. This required his traveling from country to country, trying to get visas and ships for the refugees. George Mantello supplied him with blank Salvadoran citizenship papers that paved the way for hundreds of Jews to leave Poland. One of Dr. Griffel's proudest achievements came when he helped five hundred Jewish war orphans leave Romania for France, where they were reintroduced to Jewish traditions and Jewish society.

HOPE NEVER DIES

Frustrations abounded in this work, and he encountered obstacles that would have deterred almost anyone else. Chief among them was his realization that young religious Jews sent to Eretz Yisrael were being indoctrinated by secular Zionist officials to abandon religion. Many of these youngsters had come from Orthodox families, but by placing them in anti-religious *kibbutzim*, the officials were turning them into secular Israelis.

Dr. Griffel, like many others, railed against this practice. It was this situation that led him to seek the Chazon Ish's advice. He was discouraged, to be sure. But the Chazon Ish's soothing words, and his realization that giving up would only make matters worse, kept Dr. Griffel going. Even after the D.P. camps had been shut and the refugees resettled elsewhere, he kept returning to Europe. There were still Jewish orphans here who had been adopted by Christian families during the war and had never been returned to the Jewish fold. Dr. Griffel persisted in seeking out these youngsters and trying to reclaim them for Judaism. He often encountered strong resistance, both from the adoptive parents and the Church. But every success gave him a new impetus to continue and to organize groups that would win back these unfortunate orphans around the world.

He was often asked why he devoted himself so thoroughly to *hatzalah* work, forsaking less taxing work. Didn't he miss the comforts of a quiet, peaceful life?

"Let me tell you of a true incident," he once answered. "After the Nazis invaded Hungary, many Jews tried to escape by fleeing to Romania. Usually, once they got across the border, they were safe.

"Once, though, a train filled with Jews was stopped when it arrived in Romania. The officials declared that the Jews were not going to get away with it this time. The train would be returned to Hungary, and the Jews would almost certainly be doomed.

"When the Jews in the train heard this, they took immediate action. They were prevented from leaving, so they assembled in one of the cars and began saying *Tehillim*. But as they poured out their hearts in prayer, one woman began screaming at them.

"'What good is all this praying?' she wanted to know. 'Don't you see that we're already lost?'

"One of the Jews turned to her and quoted a passage from the *Gemara*: 'Even if a sharp sword rests on your neck, never stop hoping for Hashem's loving mercy.' The woman scoffed at this, but the prayers continued.

"The train returned to the border. There it was met by Hungarian officials. They took one look and said, 'We don't want these Jews. Take them back to Romania.'

"The order was carried out, and the train was brought back to Romania. All the Jews inside survived.

"Now," concluded Dr. Griffel, "if these Jews at death's door didn't abandon their faith in Hashem, how can I even think twice about abandoning my work? How can I ever give up my belief that Hashem will help me, despite all the obstacles? That is the least I can do, and the least that these pure and holy Jews deserve."

THE CHILDREN OF SHEFFORD

REBBETZIN JUDITH GRUNFELD

Rebbetzin Grunfeld was one of the early pillars of the Bais Yaakov Seminary in Cracow, before she married and settled in England. Her heroic role in rescuing hundreds of Jewish children, the celebrated Shefford story, is related in these pages. Over the years, Rebbetzin Grunfeld has kindled a flame within hundreds and thousands of teachers and students, by her personal appearances and inspiring talks.

5   THE CHILDREN OF SHEFFORD

REBBETZIN JUDITH GRUNFELD

FROM 1939 UNTIL 1945, THE MANY STUDENTS OF THE JEWISH
Secondary School in London, as well as the hordes of refugee
children rescued by Rabbi Schonfeld from German-domi-
nated Europe, were evacuated to the safety of the English
countryside, where in the small, inconspicuous village of
Shefford a miracle occurred. The heroine of this drama was
the school's principal, a remarkable young woman by the
name of Judith Grunfeld.

A LITTLE MATTER

Early one Monday morning, Rebbetzin Grunfeld was
standing in the garden of the school in Shefford, admiring the
lovely morning and marvelling at the irony of it all. Despite
blackouts, rationing and air raids, the flowers were blooming
outside, and her students were blossoming within. A decep-
tive calm pervaded the English countryside, belying the

firestorm that was devastating Europe.

Baruch Hashem, the evacuation to Shefford seems to be working, she thought. At least, so far. All the children are safe from the bombs that are blitzing London, and things are running smoothly. She smiled with quiet satisfaction at the sounds of *davening* coming from the classrooms.

Then the message came. Rabbi Schonfeld wanted to have a word with her.

"There is a little matter in which I would like your help," Rabbi Schonfeld began.

A little matter. Rebbetzin Grunfeld knew what those words meant. She had heard that phrase often enough to know that another young Jewish life was in danger.

"You see," he continued, "there is this little girl named Sarah . . ." And he plunged into the details of the story.

Sarah's father had died when she was small, and as the threat of war loomed ever larger, her mother feared for the safety of her daughter. Hearing that Rabbi Schonfeld was evacuating children to England, she contacted him and begged him to save her little girl, who was now eight years old, and take her with him.

After arriving in London in December, 1938, Sarah was picked up from Dr. Schonfeld's school by a gentile couple offering to help, but they never brought her back. It was a time of tremendous chaos and confusion; war was about to erupt, and Sarah was lost in the shuffle.

The gentile couple placed Sarah in a non-Jewish school, and as the difficulties of keeping a determined Jewish child increased, she was shifted from one family to another, traumatized more and more by each move. When the school Sarah attended was evacuated to the country, she went with them and was placed with yet another gentile family. And then another. It took a long time for the pain to subside. Even though she was so young and so alone, she desperately clung to the cherished vestiges of her *Chassidic* background. She whispered *berachos* and refused *treif* food. And she cried for her mother.

Emotionally and physically exhausted, she knew she wouldn't bear another move. Her foster family expected her to be like the other children. As the only Jewish child in the entire town, she didn't have much choice. She would be so good, she resolved, that surely this family would let her stay. She remembered that the Chief Rabbi of England had made a special radio broadcast for the Jewish refugee children, saying, "Children, it's war time. You must do whatever your gentile hosts ask." She would try not to be difficult.

Besiyata dishmaya, Rabbi Schonfeld was finally able to relocate Sarah. He was appalled to discover that she was stranded among the gentiles in a small town called Biggleswade, cut off from the Jewish community. Realizing the spiritual danger that she faced, he immediately got in touch with Rebbetzin Grunfeld and told her the name of the village in which Sarah was staying. This was the little matter in which he needed some help.

It turned out that Biggleswade was right next to Shefford, and Rebbetzin Grunfeld immediately set out to get Sarah.

"Hello, Sarah." Rebbetzin Grunfeld smiled warmly as she looked at the young girl. "My name is Judith Grunfeld, and I live in the very next village."

Sarah couldn't help but notice how pretty and kind this stranger looked. She certainly appeared to be a very important person. But Sarah had learned to be careful. No one could be trusted.

"You know," Rebbetzin Grunfeld continued, "this is the first time I have been to Biggleswade. It looks like such a lovely place. Could you take me for a walk and show me around?"

Once out of the house, Rebbetzin Grunfeld spoke to her about the Jewish school in the next village. She talked about how, even though her students were also staying in gentile homes, they had kosher food available and were able to keep

Shabbos. And most importantly, she mentioned, they had each other.

Sarah had saved her sanity by shoving her emotions into the deepest recesses of her soul. She was now almost thirteen years old. It had been so very long since she had been in contact with fellow Jews. She remembered what it had been like in her own home in Vienna. But she could not imagine how it would be possible to live as a Jew in England. No, she had better stay put. Rebbetzin Grunfeld saw anguish beginning to seize this poor child. She hugged her gently.

"I'll come and visit again," she whispered reassuringly and left.

Rebbetzin Grunfeld could not bear the thought of losing even one Jewish child. That Sarah was no longer in physical danger did not lessen the tragedy. No, Rebbetzin Grunfeld told herself. Surely, the *Ribono Shel Olam* didn't save this child just so that she could end up like this. We'll just have to find some way to resurrect this precious *neshamah* that has suffered so much. If only Eliyahu Hanavi would come.

A few days later, Rebbetzin Grunfeld returned to visit Sarah. But this time she came with her Leah and Rosie, two very pretty, personable young girls who were the same age as Sarah. Decked out in crisp white sailor dresses, with flowers in their hair, they looked the picture of youthful exuberance. Tennis rackets in hand, they knocked on the door.

"Hi, Sarah," they chorused. "Would you like to come play with us for a little while?"

Again, once away from the house, they spoke of their special school and how truly wonderful their life was. Sarah felt herself starting to relax a little. She was not accustomed to such warmth and genuine friendship. Then, as they were about to return, Rebbetzin Grunfeld uttered a silent prayer and took Sarah aside, putting her arm around her.

"Sarah, I know that these past few years have been so very hard for you," she said. "Many of our other children have also had terrible experiences. And I know that you feel safe here. But we would like for you to come to our school. You can visit your old friends whenever you like, but I think that you will be so happy back with other children who are just like you."

Sarah just stood there. Her mind went blank. She stiffened. There was just no way. No way.

Rebbetzin Grunfeld turned Sarah around so that they faced each other. She held her firmly by the shoulder.

"But Sarah, my precious Sarah," she said very simply. "What would your dear mother think?"

These words finally pierced the wall Sarah had so carefully constructed to safeguard her memories. Her mother. She thought of her mother whom she loved so much. And she looked at Rebbetzin Grunfeld. They were alike in so many ways. Her mother had given up everything so that she could survive. Rebbetzin Grunfeld seemed to have that same determination. It was a long time before a smile could surface through the tears. But it had worked. After a while, Sarah was again saying *Modeh Ani* with all her heart.

THE CHILDREN'S TRANSPORT

From November, 1938, until the war began in September, 1939, Rabbi Schonfeld rescued hundreds of Jewish children from Austria and Germany, ferrying them safely to London on what was called "the Children Transport." But for most of these children, this was just the beginning of their ordeal.

Even though each child's story was different, many of Sarah's trials and tribulations were suffered by hundreds of her fellow refugee children. Every one had endured a sad parting that contained within it a story interwoven with pain and prayer. They came with such hope, only to find their new environment alien and hostile. Just to survive as an orphaned refugee in war-time England was difficult. Survival as a Jew seemed impossible. It was incredible that these little ones, some only five years old, managed to maintain their emotional equilibrium. But these were miracle children, released from the inferno and saved for the future. Who knew what destiny awaited them?

After *Kristallnacht*, a secular Jewish organization in London had brought over about six hundred Jewish children from Germany. Many of these children were first placed in barracks and then given to gentile families. The established Jewish community had been unwilling to respond with open arms to these poor, refugee children. Tragically, the hospitality found in the non-Jewish homes was much greater. Thus, it was not surprising that a large number were never heard from again.

For Rabbi Schonfeld this provided a bittersweet lesson. For centuries, the Jewish people had bravely chosen death *al kiddush Hashem* rather than life as a gentile. He mourned the fate of these children who were lost to their people forever. Rabbi Schonfeld now realized that saving children from the flames was only the first phase of their rescue. The remainder of the rescue operation was largely entrusted to Rebbetzin Judith Rosenbaum-Grunfeld.

A BAIS YAAKOV PIONEER

Judith Rosenbaum was born in Budapest, Hungary, her father's homeland. When she was only a year old, her parents decided to move to the more stable environment of Frankfort-am-Main, Germany, where her mother's family lived. This was the community that the Torah giant Rabbi Samson Raphael Hirsch had been able to save from the assimilation that swept through the rest of Germany. Due to his influence, the Jewish schools emphasized academic achievement within a frame-work of total Torah commitment. Young Judith excelled in both her Torah and academic studies. By the time she was twenty, armed with an advanced degree in education and her own natural talents, she was called upon to fulfill her first historic role.

The Sarah Schenirer Bais Yaakov Teacher's Seminary had just opened in Cracow, Poland, in 1923. In spite of the impoverished conditions there, word spread, and many young girls, thirsting for knowledge, flocked to the school. Sarah Schenirer and Dr. Leo Deutschlander, who helped her set up the Seminary on a sound educational basis, realized that a critical addition to the staff was needed. This very special young woman would have to be more than just an exceptional teacher. She would have to be both an inspiration and a role model. She would have to instill in these future teachers and mothers the principles and ideals that were to become the hallmark of the Bais Yaakov movement. It was Judith Rosenbaum that Moreinu Rav Yaakov Rosenheim, the head of World Agudath Israel, recommended as being equal to the task.

Arriving in Cracow in 1925, Judith stayed on, except for brief periodic interruptions, until 1932 when she got married. She came to be called Frau Doktor with much respect and affection. This young pedagogue would leave a deep imprint not only on a generation of seminary students, but also on future generations of Bais Yaakov students the world over. She was truly one of the pillars of this pioneer teachers' seminary, and her contributions have become legendary. But Judith was to also gain much more from her experiences.

During the breaks in the teaching schedule, Judith em-barked on fundraising tours. Alone and unknown, she trav-elled to London, Paris, Alsace and many other European Jewish centers. She tried to convince others of the urgent need to support the Bais Yaakov movement that was so successfully teaching these young Jewish women how to preserve their *Yiddishkeit* regardless of the challenges that would confront them. Even when the affluent Jewish businessmen she approached did not appreciate the importance of her work, she still persevered. She just changed her tactics. Who could refuse to provide blankets, clothing and food—the most basic necessities—to young Jewish girls? Sometimes it worked. She would return to her room, wash out her blouse, gloves and collar, and prepare herself for yet another gruelling day.

Judith Rosenbaum had acquired a worldly sophistication and wisdom far beyond her years. As extraordinary as her achievements had been to date, she realized, even at this early stage of her life, that even greater things would be expected of her. She could not have envisioned exactly what the Almighty had in store for her, but she wanted to prepare herself as best she could.

She returned to Germany in 1929. Wanting to earn additional credentials and expertise that would lend prestige to the Bais Yaakov movement for those girls who would otherwise have been inclined to attend secular schools, she completed her doctorate. Soon thereafter, she married Rabbi Dr. Isidore Grunfeld, who would also make a distinguished contribution to his people, both as a *dayan* and author.

One day, as Judith and her husband were walking down the street, they were forced to quickly jump aside. A Nazi procession marched by singing, "When Jewish blood drips down the knife, then we'll be doubly strong." The next morning, with only his attache case in hand, Rabbi Grunfeld walked to the train station as if it were just another day. A few hours later, carrying a small overnight bag, Judith took the same route. It was 1933, and they left Germany for good.

Rabbi Grunfeld had been a lawyer by profession and wanted to set up his law practice in Eretz Yisrael. But this required a proficiency both in the English language and British law. Thus a decision, clearly guided by the *Yad Hashem*, was made for Rabbi Grunfeld to go to school in England "for just a year." The Grunfelds arrived in London as homeless refugees who could barely speak a word of English. Rabbi Grunfeld found a job as a "house *rebbe*" tutoring a young boy, and Judith found a full-time teaching position at the Jewish Secondary School that had recently been founded by Rabbi Schonfeld.

PRINCIPAL OF THE SCHOOL

"Mrs. Grunfeld!" one of her young charges whined in dismay one day in the school. "Simon is cheating!"

Rebbetzin Grunfeld had no idea what the word cheating meant, but she looked at both boys sternly and said, "I know!"

Fortunately, her bluff worked, and the boys were silenced. But that evening, with dictionary in hand, Judith added yet another word to her rapidly expanding vocabulary. Her talents as an educator were immediately recognized and utilized. By 1935, she had already been promoted to the position of principal. Her duties were daunting, but they were to expand even further.

By 1938, events in Europe were such that Rabbi Schonfeld felt compelled to devote every ounce of his energy to his rescue efforts, and in November, he brought his first transport of two hundred children to England. This meant that Rebbetzin Grunfeld not only had full responsibility for the school, but now another dimension was added to her role. Someone had to help with these young refugee children that Rabbi Schonfeld had been able to save. Rebbetzin Grunfeld welcomed them with open arms. She became Rabbi Schonfeld's partner in rescue. He would bring these children to London, and she would take over from there. As immense a task as this was, this, too, was merely a prelude to what was to come.

Both in school and out, it was to Rebbetzin Grunfeld that the children and teachers alike would turn for solace and guidance. Not only could she speak their language, she could also empathize with their plight. More and more refugee families were flooding into England, and more and more children, frightened and forlorn, were brought over. For many, it was the kindness and Jewishness of the school that provided them with the only familiarity and stability they would find in this strange new setting. Rebbetzin Grunfeld saw to it that all were accommodated. Even though the newcomers could not speak a word of English, their strong background in both secular and religious subjects enabled them to adjust to the curriculum. And with a motivation that only new immigrants possess, they rapidly became an integral part of the student body.

Even though the school managed to run smoothly, the situation outside England continued to deteriorate. Prime Minister Chamberlain of England had declared that "Herr Hitler is a reasonable man who wants peace." Rebbetzin Grunfeld knew better. She had not only seen the Nazi menace first-hand, when she had witnessed the Nazi march together with her husband, but she had listened as the Jewish refugees attempted to describe the indescribable. The school staff maintained a "business as usual" attitude, but in the pits of their stomachs they were constantly aware that their Jewish brethren across the Channel were enduring untold suffering.

"PIED PIPER TOMORROW"

By August of 1939, the threat of war seemed imminent, and the British government began to ready the population for the coming conflict. Gas masks were distributed and supplies stockpiled. Fearful of possible Nazi bombings of London, the British government ordered that school children, including those in Rabbi Schonfeld's school, be evacuated to small villages in the countryside. Rebbetzin Grunfeld realized this meant uprooting the youngsters once again and housing them with non-Jewish strangers.

As principal, Rebbetzin Grunfeld was in charge of implementing the evacuation plan for her school. Each child was given a rucksack filled with the barest necessities, and leaflets were distributed detailing how the operation should proceed. Each day the children had to come prepared—just in case.

One day, Rabbi Schonfeld summoned the children to an assembly.

"You'll be away from London for a while," he told them, "and I hope it will be a short while indeed. I expect there will be difficulties, and you will find yourselves among people of different religions. But if you remember that you belong to a proud nation, that you must at all times represent the Jewish ideal, then I know all will go well. Here is a test to prove your loyalty to your dear parents' faith!

"One major problem you will face is *kashrus*. Many of your hosts will not understand what kosher food is, so until you have a chance to explain things to them, you'll have to tell them that you are a fish-eating vegetarian. Even if you and your hosts don't always agree, you should always treat them with the greatest respect. That is the mark of a true *ben Torah* or *bas Torah*. By acting in this way, you will create a real *kiddush Hashem*.

"One more thing. If you happen to hear anyone say anything against the Jews, don't let it upset you. Always remember that Jews have a glorious past and that with your help we will have a glorious future, too. You, my children, are the shining hope of tomorrow's world, and Hashem is with you."

On Thursday afternoon, the code words appeared: "Pied Piper tomorrow." Pied Piper tomorrow. It was a nationwide signal for schools to be evacuated to the countryside. The words resounded over and over. This time Rebbetzin Grunfeld had to sit down. So many of these children had endured so much. And now to be transported to an unknown destination yet again? And who knew for how long? She wondered how it could be done. There were now four hundred and fifty children, aged five to seventeen. Not to mention the teachers and her own three little ones. As she faced this new challenge, she prayed for strength.

By six o'clock Friday morning, September 1, 1939, everyone was assembled and ready to go, accompanied by the *sifrei Torah*. Even though the atmosphere was that of a school outing, the serenity of the English countryside completely escaped Rebbetzin Grunfeld. As the train sped along, she had much to think about. These weren't just ordinary school children. They were Orthodox Jewish children. How could they possibly survive in gentile homes? What would they do about *Shabbos* and *kashrus*? How would she ever recreate the Jewish atmosphere the refugee children so desperately needed?

Her thoughts were suddenly halted by the screeching brakes. All the children and their group leaders disembarked and were boarded onto eight separate buses. Before she knew it, Dr. Grunfeld and her group had arrived in the village of Shefford, in the township of Bedfordshire. The others were sent to four neighboring villages. Awaiting them in the town square were the assembled populace, all decked out in their Sunday best.

These simple but kind-hearted people were eager to serve their country by welcoming the school children into their homes. Mrs. Mitchell took four little girls in tow. The rector's wife welcomed seven grown boys. Mr. Taylor, who owned the laundry, unhesitatingly agreed to give lodging to an entire family of eight displaced children, ranging in age from seven to seventeen.

From little country dwellings to larger farm houses,

along the main street and down by the bridge, the children were escorted. The parson, the vicar, the grocer, the baker, the garage owner, the postman, the milkman, the antique dealer and the chimney sweep all had volunteered to make room in their hearts and their homes for the new arrivals. In short order, the square was emptied.

A DIFFICULT ADJUSTMENT

Now Rebbetzin Grunfeld had to get busy in earnest. *Shabbos* was just a few hours away, and Rabbi Schonfeld had just arrived to set up a temporary facility in the town hall. As she looked around the small room that had so graciously been allotted to her, she worried about the scenes that were surely taking place in home after home as the villagers discovered that their new guests were "different."

And indeed these scenes were taking place. The foster families had gone to so much trouble to make their new charges feel at ease. They were so kind and friendly, that even the most fearful little ones began to feel better. They saw the gardens and the chickens, and their modest but cozy bedrooms. They were genuinely grateful that conditions were not worse. But the problems had just begun.

Figuring that everyone would be famished from their journey, each host had prepared as lovely a meal as they could provide. Naturally, all the food was *treif*. The women, who had worked so hard, waited anxiously for their hungry guests to enjoy every bite. Instead, everyone just sat there. The awkwardness was further heightened when the children refused to explain their strange behavior. Some managed to murmur a "thank you anyway," but most were ill-equipped to respond at all. The villagers had expected London school children they would be able to raise as their own. Instead, they found they had foreigners who couldn't even speak English.

In a very short time, an atmosphere of aggravation permeated the community. By the end of *Shabbos*, it had gotten worse.

"Johnny," the farmer had called politely. "Would you just switch on that light for me while I get this bucket?"

"Jackie," Grandma sweetly asked. "Could you just set that kettle on the stove while I prepare something to drink?"

The story was the same all over. These dear precious children, who were so eager to please, were confronted for the first time in their lives with the painful situation of being unable to comply. They also lacked both the language skills and the maturity to explain their dilemma diplomatically. Over the backyard fence and at the post office, the neighbors congregated to complain about their unappreciative evacuees. Annoyance and anger were gaining momentum all around.

For most of these villagers, the word Jew evoked unpleasant images born of old prejudice. They were also upset at hearing a language that sounded so much like German. This only further aroused suspicions that perhaps these strangers were really Nazi spies. It was natural to dislike that which was so dissimilar. When ignorance and superstition were added, an ugly prejudice rapidly surfaced. The truth is that these good Christian people were just plain disappointed. They had hoped to bolster their Sunday school and rejuvenate the church choir. Instead, they felt that the government had cheated them by dumping these foreigners in their laps. A revolt was brewing, and an exodus back to London was planned!

Rebbetzin Grunfeld immediately grasped the urgency of the situation. Gathering her staff, she made sure each and every home was visited. Dr. Grunfeld was at her finest. Her charm and graciousness won everyone's admiration. She gently explained that the children had indeed come from different backgrounds. Even those born and raised in Britain still adhered to their religious laws and customs. She then carefully detailed the dietary laws and how vegetables and fish could be prepared. She beseeched the families to be tolerant, assuring them that the day would come when they would be rewarded for their efforts.

That day did come, but it took time. And some adjustments were more difficult than others. Sometimes, there was an almost humorous side to it.

"Dr. Grunfeld," Mrs. Smythe had begun. "I must speak to you about Harry." She was carrying a large, hot, covered dish.

"Well, of course," Rebbetzin Grunfeld replied.

"Dr. Grunfeld, I prepared this seafood just like I am supposed to, and Harry still refuses to eat it!"

Rebbetzin Grunfeld had to stifle a laugh as she removed the cover to reveal a steaming red lobster.

Eventually, most of the initial culture shock subsided, and the families became very attached to these immaculately groomed Jewish children who were so polite and well-behaved. The children came to be respected for their religious steadfastness and to be loved in spite of the differences. Before long, the grocer began stocking kosher margarine so that his customers could provide their guests with something other than dry bread. *Tzitzis* could be seen hanging with the family wash, and in house after house, on Friday nights, it was the gentile guardian who quietly walked into the bedroom and switched off the light so that the children could sleep more peacefully. Rebbetzin Grunfeld had been able to neutralize the most negative aspects of these non-Jewish homes, but so much more still had to be done.

THE SHEFFORD SCHOOL

The key to Jewish survival has always been Jewish education in a Jewish environment, even in time of war, and even in places like Shefford. Or perhaps, *especially* in time of war and *especially* in places like Shefford. It was not enough just to come out of it alive. These precious *Yiddishe neshamos* who had been spared the fate that took the lives of more than one million of their young sisters and brothers now had a special mission to fulfill. They had a heritage to preserve, both for themselves and for their people.

It was to this task, the establishment of a Jewish school in Shefford, that Rebbetzin Grunfeld devoted herself with a frenzy, with the asistance of a devoted, competent, caring staff. Eventually, over six hundred children would pass through the doors of the Jewish school in Shefford. By now, the war had begun. Even though they were far away from London, they could still hear the terrible bombings. Nevertheless, the framework for a makeshift school was begun.

They finally arranged to use an empty theater. It had taken a superhuman effort, but it was working. Ten different lessons were held simultaneously in ten different groups, while at the same time dinner for another two hundred was being cooked in yet another corner. And then a catastrophe happened. The theater was destroyed by fire. There were other setbacks as well. But they were finally able to settle into an old schoolhouse on Clifton Road. Then some living quarters for a few students were obtained nearby, and the White House on North Bridge Street became the *bais midrash*.

Soon, a full-fledged school was in operation with a complete secular and religious curriculum. *Chumash, Navi, dikduk* and other studies were covered. There was also a special *mussar shiur* given, as well as a Jewish philosophy class that discussed the proper behavior to display under these singular conditions.

A prefabricated structure was erected right next to the school building. This served as a kosher dining hall that not only provided the children with kosher food but also with a place for camaraderie and group get-togethers. Rebbetzin Grunfeld couldn't replace the families they had left behind, but she had at least enabled them to have each other. They *davened*, learned, ate and played together.

At every opportunity, Rebbetzin Grunfeld was there to inspire and guide her students. It was difficult to maintain a temporary situation on a long-term basis, but somehow it would have to be done, especially since no one knew when the war would be over. Rebbetzin Grunfeld called all of the students together for an assembly.

"We celebrate today the completion of one full year's work as a community in Shefford . . . One year is a long time in your young lives . . . Those of you who did not know one word of English, now say 'ain't it' very nicely, and those who said 'ain't it' before have now become well reared in the finesse of English language and culture!

"Hardship breeds heroism in people of superior character . . . Let us work with all our energy as if there would be a fire. In reality, there is a fire burning from one end of Europe to the other. Synagogues have been burnt down, together with *sifrei Torah, yeshivos* and *batei midrashim*. Let us now, every one of us, assist in the brave work of rescue, to save from the fire what can be saved by strengthening this community which you yourselves have founded.

"This school community has made these twelve months of isolation rich in value, but we must continue to put our hearts and souls into it. There was a time long ago when young people had to be reminded that one day they would have to grow up. You realize already that you have to shoulder your responsibilities here and now in a grown-up world under difficult circumstances. We are proud of you."

That they were able to accomplish so much in just one year was nothing short of miraculous. Rebbetzin Grunfeld herself was a living example of the words she spoke. Through her constant and continual inspiration, this remnant of Jewish youth had indeed been able to preserve its identity.

Before long, a routine was established. The seasons changed and *Yamim Tovim* came and went, each with a special flavor that would be treasured for years.

The High Holy Days were invested with an extra sanctity. After all, these were times when battles were being fought that would decide the future of the world. The children painfully realized that they couldn't know what the next day would bring, much less the next year. On *Tisha b'Av*, it was a double exile they mourned. The tears flowed for their personal losses as well as for past national tragedies. When it was *Pesach*, they were reminded that redemption had come once before. Surely, it would come again, speedily and in their day. And *Purim* was exuberant.

"Once I observed *Purim* at Shefford, with that special feeling of togetherness," one student said years later, "every other *Purim* afterwards was a letdown."

Even the gentile community was to become aware of the Jewish calendar and its peculiar demands. One morning, as Rebbetzin Grunfeld was coming down Ampthill Road, she was confronted by the sergeant.

"Dr. Grunfeld!" he exclaimed. "There are very serious complaints against your charges!"

Her heart sank as she wondered what new predicament she now faced.

"Some of your boys—and it was the big ones, who should have known better—vandalized trees on Mr. Sedley's private estate," he continued. "For heaven's sake, can't these lads enjoy the sight of a beautiful forest without going around cutting off branches? Mr. Sedley is furious!"

Lord help me, she thought. How could she even begin to exonerate these boys who were so excited about building their *sukkos*. She thought of mentioning the relevant passage in the Bible, but she instantly realized this would get her nowhere. She would have to take another approach. This could have serious repercussions.

"Oh, sergeant," she moaned. "Whatever shall I do? I guess boys will be boys, but I must watch so many of them and

I have so much to do. How in the world can I ever appease the owner of that lovely forest . . . ?" She let her voice trail off in feigned despair.

"Now, don't you worry, ma'am," the sergeant sympathetically replied. He pitied her helplessness and immediately assumed a different posture. "Just you leave everything to me!" And in a flash, he left to carry out his civic duty.

Much to the surprise of Rebbetzin Grunfeld, he reappeared the following year. In a semi-official whisper, he informed her of a place where tree limbs could be cut "for that tabernacle of yours, which I learned about from my own sources."

There is also an interesting entry in the record of the Church Ladies' Guild that the annual Whist Drive to raise funds for the church was postponed. After all, that day was *Lag Baomer*, and the women had to take the children for haircuts.

As elated as Rebbetzin Grunfeld was with how the children had been able to safeguard their religious heritage, she was well aware that, as far as the government was concerned, her primary duty was to be the principal of a traditional educational institution. When Rebbetzin Grunfeld received official notification from the Ministry of Education that His Majesty's Inspector was coming to visit their evacuated school, she feared he would fail to understand their special needs. She held her breath when he walked in and observed the children reciting *Tehillim*. He listened as the heavily accented teachers patiently instructed their students in a variety of subjects foreign to him. He stayed for two days. Finally, he called Rebbetzin Grunfeld in for a conference.

"The Lord's blessing be with you," he began. "It has been an experience to see so much good cheer in the eyes of so many homeless children. Your heroic efforts have resulted in the most extraordinary work under the most adverse conditions."

Not only did he assist Rebbetzin Grunfeld in requisitioning materials and supplies that were so badly needed, but his glowing report helped lay the foundation for government support of the many Jewish Day Schools that were to spring up in the future.

People in the surrounding areas also marvelled at the wondrous happening that had occurred in their midst, and they were overwhelmed by the presence of Rebbetzin Grunfeld. She was a truly regal character who possessed an innate majesty that was apparent to all. Reverently referred to as "the Queen" by Jew and gentile alike, she commanded awesome respect and admiration. She was often seen coming down the road from one facility to another. When these outings would occur, the local people would sometimes stop and wave. Fortunately, word of her presence also spread to others.

One day, there was a loud knock on her office door.

"Come in!" Rebbetzin Grunfeld called out.

Much to her surprise, in walked an eight-year-old little boy who promptly walked right over to her chair.

"I want to see the headmistress," he demanded.

"Well, I am the headmistress," Rebbetzin Grunfeld explained. "What can I do for you?"

"My name is Manfred. I live in Henfrow, and I took a bus to get here. I do not live with a Jewish family, and I do not go to a Jewish school. But I am Jewish. I understand this is a Jewish school, and I think I am entitled to come." With that he sat down.

Dr. Grunfeld had to stand up and turn around as the tears welled up in her eyes. "*Ribono Shel Olam*, in whose merit was this little child given the strength to find us? Was it his mother's prayer as she *bentched licht*, or his father's *Shabbos berachah* that he should be like Ephraim and Menasheh, who were able to maintain their identity in spite of their foreign surroundings?" One thing she did know for sure. Another *neshamah* would be saved.

Another time a little girl with a round face and dimpled cheeks walked in. Her name was Peppy, and she was eleven years old. When asked why she wanted to leave the family and the school where she had been placed, she softly replied, "Is it true that you make *Kiddush* and *Havdalah* here? It's been so long since I last heard *Kiddush* and *Havdalah*." Her eyes said the rest. She soon moved in.

FOR THE DURATION

Rebbetzin Grunfeld knew that they were to remain in Shefford "for the duration," but no one had any idea of how long that would be. The years rolled past. Miraculously, the township of Shefford had been transformed into a kind of Noah's Ark, floating under divine protection, above the horror destroying the rest of the world.

One day they would have to alight and confront the wreckage, but for now, they were sheltered. There was fresh air in the fields and sunshine in the meadows. The children had found such friendship and solace amongst themselves that even the agony of waiting for mail (that for many, tragically, ceased to arrive) slowly abated. They became caught up in all the events that make up the day in a community so young and adventurous. When news came of parents who had been killed in London bombing raids, the children learned to share their sorrow and grief. They also learned to experience the comfort that comes from being together with others who share a common destiny.

Rebbetzin Grunfeld's office was tiny, but it exuded a certain warmth that made the children feel at home. This was easy to understand, for it was in this office that all their needs were attended to. This time, it was Eugene who had entered.

"Good morning, Dr. Grunfeld." Eugene beamed shyly.

"Oh, good morning, Eugene," Rebbetzin Grunfeld responded with her soft smile.

She recalled the first time the small, dark-haired child had come running to her as a very frightened, lonely, nine-year old little boy. In 1939, he had been rescued by Rabbi Schonfeld, but he showed no emotion, joy or gratitude. All he could think about was that last embrace, with his mother's tears and his father's trembling voice bidding him to be a good boy. He was haunted by that final vision of his parents, the flutter of a handkerchief waving good-bye as the train pulled out of the station. He had left behind everything and everyone he knew and loved. He had not wanted to leave Rabbi Schonfeld's side. That was until he was gently passed to Rebbetzin Grunfeld. She said she would take care of him. And she had. Even though her doctorate was in the field of education, her expertise was rebuilding shattered Jewish lives.

It was now 1943 and time to celebrate Eugene's *barmitzvah*. Rebbetzin Grunfeld wanted to make it as special as possible.

"Well, Eugene," she asked, "are you prepared to read the *parshah*?"

He vigorously nodded his head up and down.

"*Baruch Hashem!*" she said with all her heart. "I am *so* proud of you!"

For a moment, their eyes met. Neither was able to speak. But they both understood. They had both worked so hard, shouldering their own burdens. In retrospect, it seemed as if insurmountable obstacles had indeed been overcome. She still found it hard to believe that the students in her school had been able to continue with their religious studies. Who could have imagined that this child, orphaned and living amidst gentiles, would live to see his *bar-mitzvah* day? Clearing her throat, Rebbetzin Grunfeld picked up her list.

"Now let's see what else we need," she continued. The new suit had been ordered by the welfare worker, and it was ready. She had also made sure he had everything his mother would have provided, such as shoes, shirt and tie.

"And we have to arrange for some *tefillin*," she added.

"Oh, I'll get them," Eugene insisted.

"From whom?" Rebbetzin Grunfeld ventured to ask.

"From my parents, of course! They will find a way."

His eyes were so full of faith, so childlike and pure, that Rebbetzin Grunfeld just smiled. There was nothing else to say. Eugene waved good-bye and returned to class. So this had been the cherished secret that had sustained him throughout the years! Eugene knew that, no matter what, his father would surely send him *tefillin*.

Just before his *bar-mitzvah*, a teacher matter-of-factly handed Eugene a pair.

"Here, Eugene," he said. "You can use these *tefillin* until yours come from your parents."

Eugene was to have them for a very long time. Yet he was one of the fortunate ones, and when he was ultimately reunited with his parents, their joy knew no bounds. Day in and day out, as they endured unimaginable horrors, one thing had been uppermost in their prayers—that their beloved son should survive. Could they dare dream he had been whisked away to some faraway island where he would be safe and sound, where he would be cared for and nourished, where he would grow to be a *ben Torah* as well? Despite the numbers on their arms and the scars on their hearts, they now considered themselves blessed. They would be grateful to Rabbi Schonfeld and Rebbetzin Grunfeld for the rest of their lives.

TIME FOR FAREWELLS

After six long years, the war was over, and it was time to say good-bye. For six long years, this had been home, and many of the children had since become adults. In spite of the hardships and privations, Shefford had become a spiritual fortress throbbing with Jewish life. And the children had grown to love it there. The magic of those years still continues to sparkle, and relationships formed in those years continue to this day.

Sir Immanuel Jakobovitz, Chief Rabbi of England and a former Sheffordian, expressed the feeling of many of his fellow Sheffordians, in remarks made some thirty years later: "Hundreds of former Sheffordians—and in the decades that followed, thousands of their children—would look back to this experience not only as a nostalgic memory evoking the most deeply cherished reminiscences but as the formative influence on their lives, their commitments, their ambitions, their friendships . . . It is to Rabbi Schonfeld's initiative, sustained by Dr. Judith Grunfeld's competence, that we owe much of the post-war miracle whereby a generation blighted by evacuation and consigned to spiritual extinction by the prophets of doom thirty years ago, became the progenitor of a community which now counts more and greater Torah institutions, generating more intensive Jewish learning and living, than ever existed in Anglo-Jewish history."

Before boarding the buses that were waiting in that same town square, a farewell assembly was held for one last time at the school. The speaker was the one person who had governed the school's destiny during those difficult and challenging years.

Rebbetzin Grunfeld, with all her humble dignity, rose to the occasion. She movingly recounted the Shefford saga. It had been an experience of epic proportions. She gratefully thanked the community for their sacrifices which had enabled these children to survive at a time when so many others had been massacred. She assured them that even though Shefford was just a small spot on the map its fame would be spread far and wide.

For many of the children, what they faced upon their

return to the real world was more traumatic than what they had left. Once again, their lives would have to be rebuilt. Fortunately, they had been given an inner strength that would sustain them for always.

Rebbetzin Grunfeld's final remarks were addressed to them. She spoke of challenges and goals.

"We are here in this world to serve a purpose of greater importance than we ourselves are . . . We are all sons and daughters of a great eternal people chosen by Hashem for a special task in the history of mankind."

Clearly, as one of the major forces behind the Bais Yaakov movement in Poland, as a gifted educator in London and as the spiritual rescuer of the hundreds of Jewish children saved by Rabbi Schonfeld, Rebbetzin Grunfeld was one of those chosen few destined for a great historic mission. Over the years she has put in personal appearances in Bais Yaakovs all over the world, captivating and inspiring her audiences with her enthusiasm and her timeless message, and to this day she continues to be a force in Torah education.

THE HOLOCAUST

A BRIEF SUMMARY

THE HOLOCAUST

A BRIEF SUMMARY

THIS BOOK DISCUSSES EVENTS THAT OCCURRED CLOSE TO HALF a century ago. Because some readers might not be familiar with this tumultuous era, a very brief review of the history of World War II and its effects on European Jewish society is included.

After the destruction of the second *Bais Hamikdash* in the year 70 C.E., the focal point of the Jewish nation for over a thousand years was Bavel (Babylonia). This was where the *Amoraim* assembled the *Talmud Bavli* and where the *Gaonim* later served as spiritual leaders for their people. Yet, Bavel, too, went into decline. The center of Jewish life then shifted once more, this time to Europe. The countries of East and West Europe gradually became home to the majority of the world's Jews between the years 1000 and 1900 C.E.

Despite intermittent poverty and sieges of persecution, Jewish life in Europe persisted and, frequently, even flourished. Europe proved to be fertile ground for the development of many legendary Torah giants. In France, Rashi and the

Baalei Tosfos produced their remarkable commentaries on the *Tanach* and the *Talmud* over eight centuries ago. Spain experienced a "Golden Age" of Judaism during the 11th through 14th centuries, producing such outstanding sages as Rabbi Yehuda Halevi, the Rambam and the Ramban. Other Torah leaders and commentators of this general time period, from different areas, included Rabbi Yitzchak Alfasi (the Rif), Rabbi Shlomo ben Aderes (the Rashba), Rabbi Asher ben Yechiel (the Rosh) and the Rosh's son Rabbeinu Yaakov, the author of the classic *halachic* work called the *Arba Turim*.

After the Jews were expelled from Spain in 1492, Eastern Europe inherited its mantle as a prime center of Torah study and observance. Between the sixteenth and twentieth centuries, such countries as Poland, Russia, Lithuania, Hungary and Romania were home to millions of Jews. Cities like Volozhin, Slobodka, Vilna, Lublin, Pressburg and Telshe gained fame as bastions of Torah learning. A dazzling array of spiritual luminaries emerged from this environment during these five centuries, including Rabbi Moshe Isserles (the Rema), Rabbi Shmuel Edels (the Maharsha), Rabbi David ben Shmuel Halevi (the Taz), Rabbi Shabse Hakohen (the Shach), the Vilna Gaon, the Baal Shem Tov, the Baal Hatanya, Rabbi Akiva Eiger, Rabbi Yisrael Salanter, the Chasam Sofer, the Chafetz Chaim, the Gerer Rebbe, Rabbi Chaim Soloveitchik, the Belzer Rebbe and Rabbi Chaim Ozer Grodzenski, among many others. The countries of Western Europe—England, Germany, France and Italy—also produced outstanding *kehillos*, vibrant Jewish communities and such major religious leaders as Rabbi Samson Raphael Hirsch and Rabbi Nosson Adler. *Chassidus*, the *Mussar* movement and the Yiddish language all blossomed in Europe.

There were major problems during these centuries, to be sure. Vicious anti-Jewish outbursts were among the worst of them. Throughout the years, European Jews had to cope with the heartache produced by the Crusades, the blood libels, the restrictions of ghetto life, the Cossaks, the pogroms and numerous expulsions. Many Jews were brutally killed by their tormentors. A large number, given the option of converting to Christianity, chose instead to go to their deaths *al kiddush Hashem* (glorifying G-d's Name).

Yet, for all the sorrows and tragedy, the Jews on the whole retained their hope for a better future and maintained their faith in Hashem. If conditions were often depressing—if they faced poverty, hunger and hatred—then tomorrow would see an improvement. A government official might issue threats now, but bribes and pleas might make him change his mind next time. And if Jews were occasionally banished from one place, there would always be another haven somewhere to which to go. So, for centuries, Europe's Jews remained steadfast in their allegiance to *Yiddishkeit*. They had their different customs and cultures, but they stood essentially united in their devotion to Hashem and Torah, and in their yearning for *Mashiach* to lead them back to Eretz Yisrael.

By the nineteenth century, some Jews felt that the era of redemption had already arrived. A spirit of independence, equality and progress, sparked by the French Revolution and spread by Napoleon's conquests of much of Europe, had kindled the promise of better times ahead. And, in fact, several Western European countries did officially grant the Jews political and social freedom, in varying degrees. Heartened, these Jews foresaw a day when they would be accepted as complete equals by their non-Jewish neighbors. It was this feeling that spurred the *haskalah* ("enlightenment") movement that attracted many Jews in both East and West Europe during the 1800s.

The leaders of the *haskalah* felt that customs and clothing that differentiated Jews from non-Jews were a nuisance. They thought that if they stood out, they would never achieve their ultimate goal—gaining complete equality in non-Jewish society. The truth, as they were to discover eventually, was that the non-Jews often rejected these "modern" Jews even more vehemently than they did their Orthodox brethren.

Nevertheless, the "enlightened" Jews still persisted in their attempts at assimilation in order to be accepted. Some went so far as to convert to Christianity. Many more thought they could secure equality if they "reformed" Judaism, by discarding traditions that were no longer "fashionable" in society. In the words of some, they "attempted to be a Jew at home and a man in public" (though many didn't keep Jewish laws at home, either). Therefore, when many German Jews, for instance, were asked to prioritize their identities, they said, "We are Germans first, and Jews second."

The European Torah community was further shaken by the effects of World War I, which lasted from 1914 to 1918. This extremely bloody conflict pitted Germany and her allies against England, France, Russia (until 1917) and, during the war's final year, the United States. Jews fought loyally on both sides and suffered mightily. But aside from individual losses, there was a widespread disruption of spiritual life. Many Jewish communities, including their *shuls* and *yeshivos*, were heavily damaged and forced to relocate during the conflict. (For instance, because of the Russian Czar's paranoia about Jews, he suspected all of them of being German spies, because they spoke Yiddish. Therefore, within a matter of days, he had almost all Lithuanian Jews transported into the interior of Russia.) The regular routine of Orthodox Jews was severely shaken. In addition, aid from America was cut off during the war, and poverty and misery abounded. And the war saw the establishment of Communism in Russia, a force that was bitterly opposed to all religions, especially Judaism.

Nevertheless, within a few years of the war's end, prospects for a brighter future grew. Secular Jews in Western Europe continued to pursue assimilation as a means of seeking an end to discrimination. Others placed their faith in such secular nationalistic movements as Zionism and Socialism.

Torah-true Jews, on the other hand, maintained their traditional approach of hastening the era of the *Mashiach* through re-established *yeshivos* and religious centers, as well as the newly-flourishing Bais Yaakov movement. Despite hardships, few Jews had reason to doubt that Europe, which had been their home for almost a thousand years, would remain the center of Jewish life for centuries to come.

The Second World War changed the situation drastically.

By the time the war ended in 1945, six million European Jews were dead—including at least two million Orthodox Jews. This represented over one-third of all the Jews in the world at that time. Many of the surviving European Jews, after being forced to live in Displaced Persons (D.P.) camps in Germany for a while, fled to Eretz Yisrael, the United States, or some other non-European country. Jewish communities that had existed for centuries were gone, and *shuls* and *yeshivos* that had been maintained for so long with such devotion were demolished. Only their ruins remained as evidence of the glory that once had been.

The country responsible for this change was Germany. After its defeat in World War I, Germany had been stripped of some of its territory and forced to pay huge fines to the victorious Allies. The Germans, a proud nation, were bitter about this humiliation. The world economic depression of the 1920s and 1930s and the virtual collapse of the German currency—plus the inability of their weak government to deal with it—further blackened their mood. There were armies of unemployed Germans, unable to pay the millions of German marks needed to buy a simple loaf of bread. They were, therefore, ready to heed the glowing promises of a great future made by Adolf Hitler and his Nazi Party, a fascist group with a philosophy of supreme power for the state.

Hitler, a failed house painter who had been gassed in World War I, was a spellbinding speaker. His bold vows to restore Germany to its former glory gained much attention. In his book *Mein Kampf* (My Struggle), he claimed that Germany's defeat in the war had been caused by traitors in the nation's ranks, especially the Jews. They were foreigners out to control Germany's economy, he insisted, and he accused them of contaminating German society. He also identified Jews with the Bolsheviks and Communists, then his bitter enemies.

In his attacks, Hitler ignored the fact that a hundred thousand German Jews had fought bravely and loyally in World War I, and that they were among the most productive citizens of the country. Because of their prominence and their minority status, the Jews made convenient scapegoats. Many Germans were jealous of the Jews' success. They resented both the Jews' entry into German society and their domination of certain fields, like medicine and law.

The Nazis took full advantage of these negative feelings and blamed the country's problems on the Jews. "Remove them from positions of power," said the Nazis, "and Germany will once again be great!" And the German people drank in these absurd claims.

Through clever political maneuvering (and despite the fact that the Nazis never gained a majority of the free vote), Hitler became leader of Germany in 1933. He immediately began carrying out his promised threats against his enemies, particularly the Jews. Jewish government officials (and later other Jews, too) lost their jobs; Jewish shops and businesses were boycotted and closed; Jewish books were burned; and Jews were taunted and beaten in the streets.

In 1935, Germany passed the Nuremberg Laws, which officially took German citizenship away from Jews and deprived them of their rights. As part of this law, a Jew was legally defined as anyone who had had even one Jewish grandparent. Suddenly, those German Jews who had sought to escape their Jewish identity by converting or assimilating became fully Jewish in the German people's eyes. They, like their more observant fellows, found themselves the victims of indiscriminate attacks by members of Hitler's brutal police force, the Gestapo. And since the government was behind these provocations, the Jews' protests fell on deaf ears.

Hitler was now the supreme dictator, the *Fuhrer* of Germany. Yet he was not content with just this. He sought to bring Germany to new heights of glory and thirsted for greater power on the world scene. Ignoring the restrictions laid down by the Versailles Treaty that had ended World War I, he built up a huge, powerful army, the mightiest army in Europe. In 1938, his troops forced Austria to agree to an *Anschluss*—a union—with Germany. Hitler quickly saw to it that the anti-Jewish laws of Germany now applied to that country as well. As a result, the mad rampages and *shul* burnings of *Kristallnacht* in November, 1938, occurred in Austria as well as Germany.

That same year, at a conference in Munich, England and France agreed to let Hitler take over a part of Czechoslovakia called the Sudetenland, where many native Germans lived. They naively hoped that this would satisfy Hitler, and England's Prime Minister Neville Chamberlain rashly said, "I believe this is peace for our time." However, Hitler's world conquest was just beginning. A few months later, the Nazis gobbled up the rest of Czechoslovakia as well. This showed the Allies that giving in to Hitler would only whet his appetite for further conquests.

By now, both Italy (under the fascist dictator Benito Mussolini) and Japan had joined with Germany to form what were called the Axis Powers. (It should be noted that the leaders of Italy and Japan did not generally share Hitler's obsessive hatred of the Jews and often declined to follow his lead in persecuting them.) Hitler also gained another (temporary) ally as well. Although Germany and Communist Russia, led by Joseph Stalin, had long been bitter rivals, in August, 1939, they stunned the rest of the world by signing a non-aggression treaty. Each country promised not to attack the other, and they would both share in the spoils of war. This gave Hitler the freedom to invade Poland without the threat of Russian retaliation. Despite warnings from England and France, that is exactly what he intended to do.

The Second World War began on September 3, 1939, two days after Germany's attack on western Poland. Ten days later, Russia invaded eastern Poland, and that beleaguered country was then divided between Russia and Germany. The United States remained neutral, leaving England, France and other European nations to carry the main burden of the battle against the Nazis.

However, after a lull in the fighting, the Germans proved their military superiority over their rivals. Employing "blitzkrieg" methods that used tanks and planes in a carefully planned program of brutality, they bombarded nations into submission. With stunning speed, the Nazis rolled over one European country after the other. By the end of 1940, Denmark, Holland, Norway, Belgium and even France itself were under Nazi control. (Northern France was occupied by German troops. The unoccupied south was governed by the pro-Nazi Vichy government.)

Greece and Yugoslavia fell in 1941; and Hungary, Romania, Bulgaria and Slovakia (formerly part of Czechoslovakia) all set up pro-Nazi governments. Finland was taken over by Russia, and Switzerland, Sweden, Spain and Turkey declared their neutrality. Only England, under the bold leadership of Winston Churchill, continued to fight on in Europe, and only the brave efforts of British pilots in the Royal Air Force prevented a German invasion of that country. These rapid conquests brought hundreds of thousands of Western European Jews under Nazi auspices.

Then, on June 22, 1941, Germany suddenly abandoned its non-aggression pact and launched a surprise attack on Russia. The drive against the Russians was at first extremely successful. The Nazis overran the western part of the country, coming within twenty miles of capturing the Russian capital of Moscow. They also took eastern Poland from Russia in the process.

These rapid German advances drew millions of additional Jews into Nazi hands. Now most of Eastern European Jewry—including Poland's three and a quarter million Jews (fully ten percent of the country's population) and over two million Russian Jews—were at the Nazis' mercy. The Nazis encouraged the non-Jewish population of each country to vent their natural anti-Jewish hatred against the defenseless Jews. In many countries, the population didn't need much prodding. (In Romania, for instance, members of the native Iron Guard viciously beat and killed thousands of Jews. And in Vichy France, one hundred thousand Jews were turned over for deportation by Nazi collaborators without much hesitation.) To make attacks against Jews even more palatable, the Nazis promised local gentiles the Jews' confiscated homes and wealth.

The Nazis themselves were now free to direct their own undiluted venom against these Jews.

Up to 1941, the Nazis did not have a clear-cut plan to murder all of Europe's Jews. The goal, to be sure, was to make greater Germany "*Judenrein*," free of Jews. However, from 1933 to 1941, the preferred method of doing so in most cases was to expel or scare away the Jews rather than to kill them. About half of Germany's three hundred fifty thousand Jews managed to flee during this time. But the question remained: Where were these persecuted Jews to go? Few countries were willing to take them in. With the entire world now at war (following the entry of the United States in December, 1941, after the Japanese attack on Pearl Harbor), free emigration came virtually to a halt.

With millions of Jews now under their control, and no one willing to take them, the Nazis came up with monstrous schemes to dehumanize and destroy them.

Among the first steps taken in the process of eliminating Jews was herding them into abominable ghettos. Jews were forced to leave their homes and were resettled in crowded, filthy, hellish confined areas that they could leave only on penalty of death. There were over two hundred of these ghettos throughout Europe, including those in Warsaw, Vilna, Cracow and Lodz. Some were run by Jewish Councils (*Judenrats*), appointed by and under the tight control of the Nazis. All had horrid conditions. Overcrowding, starvation and rampant disease were commonplace.

In the Warsaw Ghetto, at the peak of its occupation, some five hundred thousand Jews were shuttered up within a few square city blocks. Sometimes, twenty people had to share a single room. The meager food available provided for only *one-tenth* of the normal calorie requirements in some ghettos. In Warsaw, at the end, the food ration consisted of two pounds of bread, nine ounces of sugar, three ounces of jam and two onces of fat per person each *month*.

Considering this, as well as the freezing winters and the lack of fuel and warm clothing, it is no wonder that thousands of Jews were found dead—frozen or starved—each month. However, the Nazis still had even more sadistic plans for those still alive in the ghettos.

With the invasion of Russia in 1941 came a terrifying new approach. The Nazis sent groups of mobile murder units called *Einsatzgruppen* to roam the occupied areas. These well-armed teams gathered up groups of defenseless Jews and shot them down in cold blood. Often, the victims were forced to dig their own graves before being machine-gunned to death. At Babi Yar, outside Kiev, for example, thirty-four thousand Jews were brutally murdered in this way within two days. In all, a million and a quarter Jews were massacred by the *Einsatzgruppen*.

However, this method of disposing of Jews was too "messy and inefficient" for some Nazi leaders. In January,

1942, at a meeting in Wannsee, Germany, top-ranking Nazis decided to quietly finalize what came to be euphemistically called the "Final Solution to the Jewish Problem." This was a camouflaged way of stating that they planned to murder all remaining European Jews. The method chosen was to gas the Jews at death camps located throughout the continent.

The top-secret plan was developed with cunning German efficiency. First, Jews were rounded up in stages throughout Europe and deported. (In the ghettos, the deportations were made easier by the fact that the Jews were already grouped together.) When sending off the Jews, the Nazis assured them that they were being "resettled to labor camps in the East." If they worked hard, they would eventually be freed. However, after being shipped in packed "cattle trains" that were locked shut, the Jews arrived to find themselves in twilight zones of pure terror.

In Auschwitz-Birkenau, they were immediately subjected to life-and-death "selections," usually determined by the notorious Dr. Josef Mengele with a motion of his finger. Those who could work were directed to the right, and weaker ones—including the elderly, women and children—to the left. SS guards then hurried the latter to the "shower rooms," where poisoned gas killed them immediately. After any gold in their teeth was extracted, their bodies were burned in crematoria. The process proceeded like clockwork. Ten to twenty thousand could be murdered daily.

In some death camps, almost everyone was killed immediately. In Auschwitz-Birkenau and other such camps, those left alive after the first selections were forced to take part in unbearable slave labor under subhuman conditions. Soon they were almost living skeletons. Most of these eventually succumbed to disease or hunger, or they were killed by guards when they could no longer work. There were also hideous, sadistic "medical experiments" that tortured, mutilated and killed many inmates. (Non-Jewish enemies of the Nazis were also subjected to these persecutions, but in smaller numbers and without many of the humiliations doled out to the Jews.)

The Nazis were proud of these death camps, including Treblinka, Sobibor, Belzec, Chelmo and Auschwitz-Birkenau. It was in these camps that millions of Jews perished—two million in Auschwitz-Birkenau alone.

Eventually, it became clear to many Jews in the ghettos that the Nazi claims that Jews were being sent to mere labor camps were vicious lies. Deportation, they realized, meant death. In April, 1943, some Jews still alive in the Warsaw Ghetto decided that further attempted deportations would be resisted. The odds were emphatically against them. They were weak, had almost no arms and hadn't been trained for fighting. Yet, when the Nazis came to take away the seventy thousand inhabitants of the ghetto, they resisted. As the Nazis entered the ghetto, they were stunned to find themselves coming under fire. In panic, they retreated. Later, they returned with reinforcements, and the battle continued. The resisters put up a fierce struggle, which continued for a full month. It was only by setting the ghetto on fire that the Nazis squelched the revolt.

There were other revolts as well, in both ghettos and concentration camps. In Sobibor, for instance, the prisoners staged a mass break-out. Many were killed, but a number managed to escape to the forests and join the anti-Nazi partisans there. In Auschwitz, some Jewish women managed to blow up one of the crematoria. These revolts marked a heroic effort by virtually defenseless people against an army that had brought the world to its knees. Jews who joined the partisans or the anti-Nazi underground fought bravely as well.

Just as heroic, though, were the many unrecorded acts of spiritual resistance by Jews during the war. There were untold numbers of men and women who persisted in their faith by saying *tefillos*, celebrating *Yamim Tovim* and helping out their fellow prisoners—all in the face of Nazi derision. Those who dared to maintain their Judaism under the noses of the Nazis knew that they were risking death. And many did, in fact, die *al kiddush Hashem*, loyal Jews to the last. Through their insistence on remaining civilized and righteous, they thwarted the Nazis' attempts to dehumanize them and mock their *Yiddishkeit*.

The turning point of the war came in the winter of 1942. Because of unusually frigid weather, and the stubborn resistance of Russian soldiers, the invading Nazi army was turned back at the Russian city of Stalingrad. By this time, the United States had fully mobilized its vast industrial resources and military might, and was committing its full effort to fighting both the Nazis and the Japanese.

During 1943, Allied soldiers pushed back the Nazis in both Russia and Italy. Then, on June 6, 1944, an enormous force of American and British soldiers invaded Normandy on the coast of France. With this began the slow but steady process of driving the Germans back from the Western European territory they had conquered. Meanwhile, the Russians had retaken land previously lost and were advancing onto German-held territory in Eastern Europe. There were some setbacks, like the German counterattack at the Battle of the Bulge in December, 1944. However, by early 1945, the end of the war was clearly in sight.

Until the very last day, the Germans did not relent in their drive against Europe's remaining Jews. By the spring of 1944, the approximately eight hundred thousand Jews of Hungary were the only large Jewish community left still relatively intact in Eastern Europe. It seemed as if they might escape the devastation that had been visited upon their fellow Jews elsewhere. However, in March, 1944, German troops occupied Hungary. Then the chief architect of the mass Jewish murders elsewhere, Adolf Eichmann, was brought there to oversee a similar destruction of Hungarian Jewry. (After the war, Eichmann fled to Argentina. However, he was captured there by Israeli agents, brought to Israel, tried and executed in 1962.)

Using the expertise in killing that they had by now gained, the Nazis rushed to fulfill their "mission." They terrorized the Hungarian Jews and rapidly forced them into ghettos. By May 16th, they had begun shipping them from the ghettos to the death camps. Soon, Hungarian Jews were being sent to Auschwitz-Birkenau at the rate of 12,000 a day. Over half a million of them died before the deportations stopped in July.

As the Allied armies began closing in on them in 1945, the Nazis tried to cover up evidence of the death camps' existence. They started marching the remaining inmates away, no matter how dreadful their condition. Many thousands died on these forced marches. Finally, the Nazi guards fled for their lives, leaving those survivors too weak to move lying side by side with the dead.

During this time (as well as throughout the war), there were German leaders like Heinrich Himmler who were willing to barter away Jewish lives for money or for lenient treatment from the Allies. However, Adolf Hitler remained in ultimate control of German policy to the end. And he ordered his people to keep up the fight against his premier enemy—the Jews—until his death.

On April 30, 1945, as the Allied armies were battling German forces in Germany's capital of Berlin, Hitler shot himself in his private bunker. Germany surrendered unconditionally on May 8th. The Allied armies came upon the few remaining inmates of the concentration camps and were shocked by their ghastly appearance and the horror stories they told. The unbelievable had actually happened.

Despite the war's end (which became complete with Japan's surrender in August, 1945, after the United States dropped atomic bombs on two of its cities), the survivors' plight was hardly over. Many of them died of shock, disease and malnutrition even after being liberated. Thousands died of finally eating good food after being freed; their weakened bodies were just too unused to it.

Still others tried to return to their old communities, especially in Poland, only to find non-Jews occupying their homes and refusing to leave. In addition, Russian-controlled governments were gaining power in most of the Eastern European countries. The Communist antagonism towards Judaism made life very uncomfortable for those Jews who resettled there. And native anti-Semitic feeling hadn't disappeared with the Nazis' defeat. In many European towns, local residents openly told the Jews that they were sorry Hitler hadn't killed them all. In Kielce, Poland, for instance, an anti-Jewish pogrom in 1946 took the lives of dozens of Jews. In the end, most of the remaining Jews of Eastern Europe (aside from those in Russia) eventually escaped to Eretz Yisrael or the United States.

The war had devastated European Jewry. Six million Jews had perished, and the vast majority of Jewish communities (except for those in England) had been destroyed. Less than one-tenth of Poland's pre-war population remained alive; only a quarter million out of the original three and a quarter million. And many of these survived only because they had been sent to Siberia by the Russians during the war's early days. The loss was dumfounding.

Proportionately, the Torah Jews suffered far more than any other group. Fully two million of the victims had been Torah-observant Jews; ninety percent of Europe's Orthodox community had died. Almost all the great *yeshivos* and Bais Yaakov schools had been destroyed (except for the Mirrer Yeshivah, whose members had miraculously escaped to Shanghai, and remnants of a few others). The same was true of many *Chassidic* groups. The war also cost Jewry the lives of most of the great *gedolim* of the time (including Rabbi Elchanan Wasserman and Rabbi Menachem Zemba) and an untold number of budding *talmidei chachamim*, not to mention countless pious men and women of all ages. They were now gone, most without even a marker in their memory.

Also gone, except in memory and pale imitation, was the unique European style of Jewish life. No longer would voices raised in Torah learning be heard in the *yeshivos* all across Poland. No longer would the *shofar* be blared throughout Hungary. And no longer would the *lulav* be blessed all over Lithuania.

A few thousand European Torah-true Jews had survived. They would help spur a Torah revival in America and Eretz Yisrael in the years to come. But life for them would never again be quite the same.

The Jews as a people had survived the war, to be sure. Yet their world would now be forever changed. That world, too, was one of the cherished casualties of the Holocaust, a unique Jewish society that should never be forgotten.

TIMETABLE OF PRE-WAR AND WARTIME EVENTS

(Note: During the war, there was constant action in many theaters of combat throughout the world. It is impossible to mention even a majority of these developments. The listing below is restricted mainly to major events that had an impact on the lives of European Jews.)

1933 ———————————————————————————
- *January 30:* Adolf Hitler becomes Chancellor of Germany
- *March 23:* Dachau concentration camp set up for political enemies of the Nazis
- *April 1:* German Jewish shops and businesses boycotted
- *April 7:* Jews barred from civil service employment
- *April 23: Shechitah* banned in Germany
- *Spring:* Jewish professors expelled from universities

1935
- *May 31:* Jews prohibited from serving in German army
- *September 15:* Nuremberg Laws barred Jews from holding German citizenship and rescinded their rights and denied them government protection

1936
- *March 3*: Jewish doctors prohibitted from practicing medicine in government institutions
- *October 25*: Rome-Berlin Axis established by Germany and Italy

1937
- *July 1*:Establishment of Buchenwald concentration camp

1938
- *March 1:* Germany forces *Anschluss* (annexation of Austria); anti-Jewish laws now apply there as well
- *July*: Evian Conference convened in France to consider problem of refugees, but attendees offer no help to Jews
- *September 30:* At Munich Conference, England and France agree to German demands for Sudetenland in Czechoslovakia
- *October 5:* At Swiss government request, Germans mark Jews' passports with a red letter J, to prevent Jews from entering Switzerland
- *October 28:* Polish Jews in Germany expelled; Poles refuse to take them; they are stranded in frontier town
- *November 9-10*: Kristallnacht attacks on shuls and Jewish stores, as well as Jews themselves; two hundred shuls in Germany and Austria destroyed; thirty thousand Jews sent to concentration camps
- *November 12*: All Jewish retail businesses taken over by

non-Jews
- *November 15:* Jewish students expelled from German schools

1939 ——————————————————————————————
- *March 15:* Nazis take over part of Czechoslovakia. Slovakia becomes independent state with ties to the Nazi SS
- *May:* St. Louis, with nine hundred thirty Jewish passengers, denied entry into Cuba and United States
- *August 23:* Non-aggression pact between Russia and Germany
- *September 1:* Germany invades Poland
- *September 3:* England and France declare war on Germany
- *September 17*: Russia invades eastern Poland
- *September 27*: Nazi leader Heydrich orders establishment of ghettos in Poland

1940 ——————————————————————————————
- *April 9:* Germany conquers Denmark and southern Norway
- *April 27*: Nazi leader Himmler orders establishment of Auschwitz concentration camp
- *April 30*: Lodz ghetto, with one hundred sixty-five thousand Jews, is established
- *May 10*: German invasion of Holland, Belgium and France
- *June 22*: France surrenders to Germany
- *October 22*: Jews expelled from Alsace-Lorraine in France
- *November 15*: Warsaw ghetto, with half a million Jews, is sealed off

1941 ——————————————————————————————
- *January 21-26:* Hundreds of Jews killed in riots by

pro-Nazi Iron Guard in Romania
- *April*: Greece and Yugoslavia occupied by Nazis
- *June:* Pro-Nazi Vichy government in south France removes French citizenship from Jews
- *June 22*: Germany invades Russia
- *July-December: Einsatzgruppen* killing units murder a million and a half Jews in Nazi-occupied Russian territory
- *September 6*: Jews in German-held lands ordered to wear Yellow Stars
- *September 28-29*: Murder of thirty four thousand Jews at Babi Yar in Russia
- *October*: Establishment of death camp at Auschwitz-Birkenau
- *December 7-8*: Japan attacks Pearl Harbor; U.S. enters war
- *December 8:* Germans kill twenty seven thousand Jews in Riga, Russia

1942
- *January 20*: At Wannsee Conference, "Final Solution" plans are mapped out to murder all European Jews
- *March-June*: Gassing of Jews begins at Auschwitz, Sobibor, Belzec, Treblinka death camps
- *Summer*: Deportation of Polish, French, Dutch Jews to death camps
- *July*: British stop Germans at El Alamein, Northern Africa
- *December 17:* British House of Commons hears that Jews are victims of mass murder in death camps

1943
- *February*: Russians defeat German armies at Stalingrad
- *March*: Residents of Cracow ghetto deported
- *April 19-May 16:* Warsaw ghetto uprising
- *June 11*: Nazi leader Himmler orders liquidation of all

ghettos in Poland and Russia, and deportation of residents to death camps
- *July 25*: Italian dictator Mussolini overthrown
- *August 2*: Revolt in Treblinka death camp
- *October 14:* Revolt in Sobibor death camp
- *Fall*: Liquidation of ghettos in Vilna, Riga, Minsk

1944
- *January 22*: Roosevelt creates War Refugee Board to save Jews
- *January 27:* Russians end German siege of Leningrad
- *March 19*: Germany occupies Hungary
- *May 15*: Deportations of Hungarian Jews begins
- *June 6*: Allies land at Normandy, France
- *Spring*: Russians drive German forces back
- *July 24*: Russians liberate Majdanek concentration camp
- *Summer*: Liquidation of Lodz and Kovno ghettos
- *August 23:* Pro-Nazi government in Romania overthrown
- *October 7:* Crematorium blown up by inmates at Auschwitz
- *October 18:* Slovakian revolt against Germany fails
- *October 31*: Deportation of Slovakian Jews to Auschwitz

1945
- *January 17*: Warsaw falls to Russian armies
- *January 17:* Evacuation of Auschwitz and beginning of death march
- *January 26*: Auschwitz liberated by Soviet troops
- *April 6-10:* Death march of inmates in Buchenwald
- *April 12*: President Roosevelt dies
- *April 13:* American troops liberate Buchenwald camp
- *April*: Invasion of Germany by Allies
- *April 30*: Hitler commits suicide
- *May 8*: Germany surrenders
- *August 14:* Japan surrenders